Contents

H0329275

Abbreviations and symbols

abbr	abbreviation
adj	adjective
AE	mainly or exclusively American English
IrE	mainly or exclusively Irish English
BE	mainly or exclusively British English
cf.	Lat. *confer* = compare; see
derog	derogatory
e.g.	Lat. *exempli gratia* = for example
esp.	especially
etc.	Lat. *et cetera* = and so on
fml	formal
infml	informal
l., ll.	line, lines
n	noun
p., pp.	page, pages
sb.	somebody
sl	slang
sth.	something
usu.	usually
v	verb
vulg	vulgar

Where two pronunciations of a word are given in the annotations, the first is the standard British English, the second (after the symbol ☆) the standard American English pronunciation. Regular differences in American pronunciation from the British – as for instance the [-r] after vowels – have not been given.

Dear Student,

Don't we already know most of what there is to know about Ireland? An island behind the island, endlessly green, populated by wild rebels and religious fanatics, great singers and poets? A place from which people emigrated for centuries because it was too poor to offer them anything? Where the modern world has yet to arrive, and where people always have time for a chat and a drink? These perceptions of Ireland are, of course, constructs or make up at best a very limited view, happily preserved from all sides, particularly by the tourism industry and the press. Northern Ireland, at the same time, has also long been limited in the public perception – and in schoolbooks – to a place of troubles and terror.
But there is more to Ireland as a whole and many changes have taken place in recent times, including in the relations between Ireland and Germany. In fact, you may be surprised to find how much the country has changed.
The Irish economy is no longer a worrisome weakling (though even the hearty 'Celtic Tiger', as it is called, is feeling a bit ill lately), Irish society is becoming increasingly diverse and multiracial, and changing attitudes towards the Church are having profound effects on family and religious values. And then there is Northern Ireland, where the shaky peace process gives cautious hope for a gradual return to normal life.
What do these changes look like on the everyday and personal level? How are they perceived by different sectors of the public? What effects are they having on the Irish identity? Read on and find out about these questions and more!

Gisela Holfter, Horst Dickel

MEMORIES
HELLO
MEMORIES

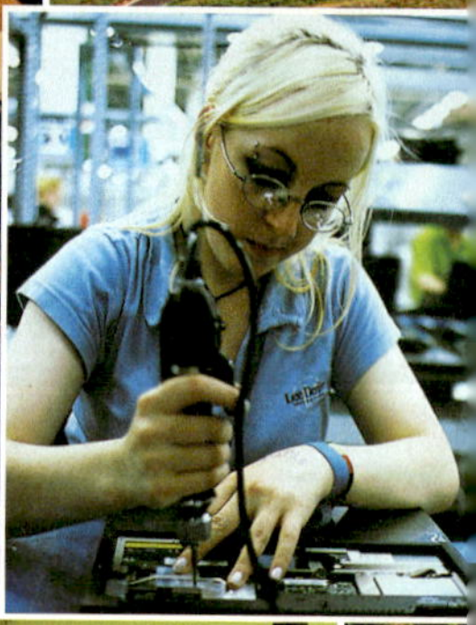

TO LET
TO LET
SOLD

GUINNESS
FITZGERALD'S

Ireland

Different images come to mind when we think of the Emerald Isle. To what extent do the pictures on these pages reflect your own perceptions of Ireland? Using these images and what you already know, write down all the words and phrases you can think of relating to Ireland. Organize them according to subjects or themes – it might help to make a mind map. Then present your perception of Ireland to the class using the words and phrases and discuss where different perceptions might come from.

Views of Two Cultures

1 Impressions of Another Land

A person's individual impressions of a foreign culture can say a lot about both the other culture as well as the culture of the individual. Irish and Germans of different ages were interviewed to find out how they perceive Germany and Ireland, respectively. Here are some of their responses.

Irish Impressions of Germany

I find that they are an intelligent, generous, helpful people, very hardworking, but they certainly find time for holiday and leisure. Their conversations have a lot more meaning than some of the superficial conversations you come across in Ireland, centred around alcohol. Having said that, I do think that the Germans should laugh a bit more. Their country is a beautiful one, efficiently run and they look after it well. You would never find yourself waiting for hours in the rain for a bus there. However I feel that as concerns towns, when you have seen one, you have seen them all.
Fiona McDermott, 21 years

The people are all very abrupt, like the people checking whether you have a valid ticket on the buses, whereas in Ireland they don't go round meticulously checking every ticket – if you flash it they just say 'Yeah'. But the public transport was much better than it is in Ireland – the buses and things came on time. And all the stations are really clean – you've got the three little bins which you can recycle everything in.
Laura Little, 16 years

Nowadays you tend to look at Germany as the United States of Europe. It is inundated with foreigners, the likes of Turks, Eastern Europeans. I mean, it is obviously the America of Europe, really. It is good and bad. And in my experience older Germans don't tend to like it a lot, which is perfectly understandable. I don't think in this country they are too open-minded about refugees as well. Younger Germans I have been talking to can't really understand that attitude.
Leonard King, 22

My mental image of Germany is chequered. Germany is a home of philosophy, theology, music, science, literature, industrial excellence and economic power. Germany has fought in very nasty European wars, been home to the Holocaust, the concentration camps, the rise of the axis, the burning of books, the pillorying of marginalised sections of society. In common with the French, the English, the Spanish and the Italians, Germany has an imperial, colonial and military history that for me invite a critical eye on her contributions to the future of Europe. A large population and economic strength needs in my view the perspective of the smaller, less powerful peoples to avoid the slide into repeating the mistakes of history.

Eoin Stephenson, 56

German Impressions of Ireland

Irland ist landwirtschaftlich sehr schön, mit freundlichen und hilfsbereiten Menschen, das Zeitverständnis unterscheidet sich enorm vom deutschen Zeitverständnis, alles geht geruhsamer, Geduld ist ganz wichtig. Die Iren haben ein entspannteres Verhältnis zum Geld was man auch am Zustand der neuen Eurogeldscheine sieht. Ein feuchtes Land in dem der Pub der einzig warme und trockene Ort ist.

Aline Dathe, 27

In Irland regnet es viel und die Leute sind freundlich und sie haben netten Akzent, besonders wenn sie vom Norden kommen. Das Bier ist besser als in England, Guinness kann man wenigstens trinken. Irland ist wesentlich teurer als Deutschland. Im Winter sind wenig Touristen da, da ist es schön, ich weiss nicht wie es im Sommer ist, wahrscheinlich unerträglich voll.

Reinhard Bäuml, 33

Ich habe noch nie so viele Löcher in den Straßen gesehen wie in Irland, für Radfahrer ist Kabul sicherer als Irland. Die Berge in Connemara übertreffen selbst die Alpen, sind viel attraktiver. Aber die Infrastruktur könnte noch sehr verbessert werden. Auch in Irland gibt es Umweltprobleme, die Plastiktüten sind überall und verstopfen sogar Gullys, so dass es riesige Überschwämmungen gibt.
Hermann Rasche, 59

5 *superficial* (derog): oberflächlich **15** *meticulous* [- '- - -] (adj): paying careful attention to every detail **16** *flash sth.* (infml): quickly show sth. **22** *inundated with sth.*: filled or occupied by so many of sth. (here: people) that one cannot deal with them all **22** *the likes of sth.* (infml): used to talk about people of a particular type or social class **32** *chequered* (BE) = (AE) checkered (adj): (usu. of a person's/country's/organization's past/history/career) having had both successful and unsuccessful periods **36** *pillorying* (n) (fml): strong public criticism of sb. **36** *marginalized* (adj): (of a person or group of people) made to feel as if they are not important or have no power or influence **43** *slide into sth.* (n): Abstieg zu etwas

1. Which of the statements did you expect and which impressions came as a surprise to you?
2. Thinking back to the collage on the previous pages and the impressions of those pictures that you discussed in class, what parallels do you see with the impressions that are voiced here? Are the views of Ireland and Germany complementary or opposite?
3. If you look closely at Leonard King's statement you will find some structures and expressions which are more often used in oral than in written English. Give at least two examples.

2 Relations Between Ireland and Germany

The following information from the website of the German Federal Foreign Office gives an official view of Germany's interaction with Ireland in a few important areas.

Right: Irish Prime Minister Bertie Ahern and German Chancellor Gerhard Schroeder during talks in Bonn in 1998.
Below: Irish President Mary Robinson with her husband Nicolas Robinson on an official visit to Berlin in December 1992.

Political Relations

The bilateral relations are traditionally friendly and problem-free. The settlement of German small and medium-sized companies in sometimes less developed regions of the country and Ireland's popularity as a travel destination have given these relations greater substance. In 1990, during its EU Presidency, Ireland contributed significantly towards creating the necessary preconditions for the reunification of Germany.

In recent years these good relations have been reflected in numerous top-level meetings and in Ireland's selection as the focus of the 1996 Frankfurt Book Fair.

Economic Relations

German-Irish economic relations are intensive. Germany is Ireland's third-largest trading partner, albeit far behind the United Kingdom and the United States. The following figures show how trade in goods has evolved over the past few years:

	Imports from Germany (in billions of €)	Exports to Germany (in billions of €)
1999	2.6	7.8
2000	3.3	9.3
2001	3.8	11.7

Irish exports to Germany fell by 5% from 1998 to 1999 while imports from Germany rose by 4%. Thanks to a strong multinational hi-tech production sector, Ireland has considerable trade surpluses with most of its trading partners. Exceptions to this rule include China, Japan, Taiwan and Singapore. Germany is the third-largest purchaser of Irish products (after the UK and the USA), as well as the third-largest supplier of imports (after the UK and the USA).

Strong trade between Ireland and Germany has benefitted both countries.

Up until around 1990 German companies for the most part established sales outlets and production sites in Ireland. After 1990, however, following the establishment of the International Financial Services Centre (IFSC), a large number of companies in the banking and insurance sectors settled in Dublin. Currently there are around 400 such companies, 40 of them from Germany. They benefit from the favourable tax situation as well as the fact that skilled personnel is still relatively inexpensive in Ireland.

The very prestigious German-Irish Chamber of Commerce has existed since 1981.

Cultural Relations

German-Irish cultural exchange is very active. Scholarship programmes (German Academic Exchange Service – DAAD, Educational Exchange Service – PAD), teacher and teaching assistant exchanges, and the debating com-

petition for secondary school students learning German are continuing to show positive development. The level of language proficiency is improving steadily in all three areas.

The vast majority of exchanges between cultural, scientific, and educational institutions in Germany and Ireland takes place directly and without any further involvement on the part of government authorities.

The most important institution for the promotion of bilateral cultural exchange with Ireland is the Goethe-Institut Dublin, which offers a widely varied programme. The association of teachers of German in Ireland is also very active.

2 *bilateral* [ˌbaɪ'lætərəl]: involving two groups of people or two countries **2–3** *settlement:* Niederlassung **13** *albeit* [ˌɔːl'biːɪt] (fml): although **19** *considerable* (fml): great in amount, size or importance **29** *insurance* [-'ʃʊər- ☆ -'ʃʊr-]: Versicherung **40** *proficiency:* ability to do sth. well because of training or practice **42** *vast:* extremely large in area, size, amount, etc.

1. Sum up the official view of the German Foreign Office towards Irish-German relations.
2. What elements contribute to the relationship between Ireland and Germany? Which of these do you find particularly important and why?
3. Can you name an Irish author, musician, pop group, politician, film or product? Together with your neighbour, try to find at least two names in each category. Share your results with the class.

The German-Irish pop group Reamonn.

Riverdance (left), the popular Irish stepdance ensemble, performs regularly to sell-out crowds in Germany.

3 A German-Irish Controversy

In an article which appeared in *Der Spiegel* in September 1998, Ireland correspondent Dirk Koch looked critically at how Irish farmers benefit from the European Union's agricultural subsidy system. Below is an excerpt from the article. When the *Irish Times* reprinted the article in English, it provoked a storm of protests in Ireland, especially in West Cork, where Koch himself lives. The *Cork Examiner* of 3 October, 1998, responded quickly with the commentary by Anne Lucey on the next page.

Brussels Is an Irish Farmer's Dream

Dirk Koch

Ireland is an island of wonders. Colourfully painted concrete statues of the Blessed Virgin can sometimes be seen moving in Ballinspittle. They have attracted hundreds of thousands of people. 'Moving rocks' jump at the harmless farmer on his return from the pub and dent his fender.

Then there is the amazing money stream. 'Jesus, the lolly flows into your pocket and you don't have to do anything,' says one Skibbereen farmer after a visit from a State farm adviser.

The man in question got to know the world through long hard years in container ships and now as a pensioner has started a cattle business. He is astonished at how easy money is thrown at him.

On inherited and leased land on the coast he has 23 cows and 23 sheep. In order to be an eligible farmer he asked the State for a herd number. That was easy. Without selling a calf, a lamb or a litre of milk he gets several thousands of pounds a year in assistance from Brussels.

'Actually, I only have to sit on my behind and watch the animals.' He lifted two fingers of his right hand, and saluted with the cap. 'Brussels is fantastic.'

'In former times we earned our money by producing food,' says a farmer from Castletownshend. 'Today we earn it by filling out subsidy forms.' The biggest problem is keeping informed about the current situation of EU subsidies.

In 1997 some 160,000 Irish farmers earned £940 million alone in direct payments from Brussels. In addition they received hundreds of millions for the sale of products at guaranteed prices.

subsidy: Subvention **2** *Blessed Virgin* ['blesɪd 'vɜːdʒɪn]: heilige Jungfrau, i.e. Maria, die Mutter von Jesus Christus **2** *concrete* ['kɒŋ- ☆ 'kɑːŋ-]: Beton **3** *Ballinspittle:* small village in County (= Grafschaft) Cork, in the south of Ireland (cf. map, inside cover) **6** *dent* (v): hollow place in a hard surface, usu. caused by hitting it **7** *fender:* Kotflügel **9** *lolly* (IrE sl): money **10** *Skibbereen:* coming from the town of the same name in County Cork (cf. map, inside cover) **17** *inherited* (adj): received from sb. when they died **17** *leased* (adj): (of property) used in return for regular payment, e.g. each month **19** eligible ['elɪdʒəbl]: fit, worthy or qualified for sth. (esp. a job or function) **29** *Castletownshend:* small village in County Cork (cf. map, inside cover)

How the Germans Found Their Lebensraum into the West

Anne Lucey

Quite apart from the glaring misrepresentation of facts, the recent article in the influential German news magazine Der Spiegel was notable for one other thing: the latent prejudice towards the Irish there is among the Germans, even by those who like the German author, live among us.

The Germans are the single biggest non-English speaking group to live among us. There are now 6,343 registered as living in Ireland and thousands more have made their home here since the last census. They started arriving here about 25 years ago, most of them to the West Cork, South Kerry and Clare-Galway areas.

Few of them came for the beauty of the people. Most of them came for that old tenet of the National Socialists of the 1930s: 'lebens-raum', living a space. No sooner do they arrive, having escaped what they do not like in Germany, than they immediately set about creating another Germany.

Only people living in West Cork and South Kerry, along the Spanish Coast, and parts of Greece are not one whit surprised by the tone of the Der Spiegel article. They are used to such remarks.

In turn, the familiar tones and slurs of the article go some way to explaining and bringing to a wider audience the depth of dislike which exists among locals for the Germans who moved in here but which, until now, has not been revealed.

The arrogance of attitude which the article betrays is one of the reasons for widespread dislike. High walls, higher gates, barking voices and the blocking of centuries-old rights of way. The German attitude to the Irish was never that of an equal. Only very recently have the German enterprises in Kerry appointed Irish people in senior positions in their hotels and factories in Kerry.

Even so it is only still a token few who are in charge in German owned enterprises here. Even today when they extend their hotels and build their houses in some of the South's most beautiful spots, in lands locals cannot afford, the materials, including even nails, are imported directly from Germany. Irish materials, like Irish labour is rarely good enough.

What really chills to the bone in the Der Spiegel article is how very near its slurs are to 19th century propaganda in British magazines about the Irish.

Superstitious oafs, cute hoors, – at one stage our heads were measured and shown to be nearer apes than any other race – is only part of it.

During the famine the influential English Punch magazine cast us as ungrateful and treacherous, unfit to govern ourselves or even to enjoy the same constitutional rights as the rest of the United Kingdom.

What the gist of the Der Spiegel article amount to are: the Irish are not good Europeans. They are cheating, lying, lazy, ignorant, conniving people.

1 *glaring* (adj): (of sth. bad) very easily seen **4** *latent* ['leɪtnt]: existing, but not yet very noticeable, active or well developed **13–14** *West Cork:* western area of County Cork (cf. map, inside cover) **14** *South Kerry:* southern area of County Kerry **15** *Clare-Galway:* two counties in the west of Ireland **16** *tenet* (fml): firm belief, opinion or dogma **24** *not one whit:* not at all, not the smallest amount **27** *slur:* unfair remark about sb./sth. **30** *local* (n): person who lives in a particular area **35** *barking* (adj): bellend
36–37 *rights of way:* permission to go over somebody's land **42** *token* (adj): pro forma, symbolisch **44** *extend sth.:* make sth. (esp. a business) cover more areas or operate in more places **51** *chill to the bone:* frighten
55 *superstitious:* influenced by old-fashioned beliefs about luck and magic **55** *oaf:* Flegel
55 *cute hoor* [kjuːt huːr] (IrE) (derog): person who uses whatever means possible to get what they want **59** *the famine* ['fæmɪn]: reference to the period between 1845 and 1850 when, as a result of failed potato crops, millions of Irish people died of hunger or disease or emigrated **60** *cast sb. as sth.:* describe or present sb. in a particular way **61** *treacherous* ['tretʃ-]: that cannot be trusted, intending to harm you **66** *cheating* (adj): acting in a dishonest way in order to gain an advantage **67** *conniving* [kə'naɪvɪŋ] (adj): behaving in a way that secretly harms others

1. What is the main message of the article excerpt from *Der Spiegel*?
2. Describe the tone of Dirk Koch's article.
3. Sum up Anne Lucey's reactions to the *Spiegel* article, as expressed in her personal comment.
4. To what extent are Lucey's claims and criticisms based on empirical facts?
5. What role do clichés about Germans play in Lucey's comment?
6. Write a letter to the editor of the *Cork Examiner* in which you express your views about Anne Lucey's article.

The mythical Irish leprechaun, a crafty elf-like figure.

From Poorhouse to Model Economy

1 Celtic Tiger Jane Black

The Irish Republic has undergone a dramatic economic transformation over the last two decades with record growth rates. Its booming economy quickly earned the nickname 'Celtic Tiger', a reference to the Asian Tigers, the five economic powers of East and Southeast Asia. This feature article explores some aspects of Ireland's astounding growth. The article appeared in November 2000 in the US online weekly *ZDNet*.

High-tech industry has helped turn the economy around.

After just four months of searching, Sheila Ryan and her boyfriend found the perfect house. Located in Bray, an Irish coastal town about 10 miles south of Dublin, the house has three modest bedrooms, a backyard and enough space for the couple's collection of scuba and biking gear. Most important, neither would have to fight Dublin's infamous traffic because Bray is on the Dublin Area Rapid Transit, the local rail line that runs into the Dublin city center.

'We were very, very lucky. We paid 125,000 pounds. The prices – just four months later – are now up to 160,000 pounds for the same sort of house,' says Ryan, a 28-year-old public relations manager at ISI, a Dublin multimedia company.

The growing Celtic Tiger: a political cartoon from the *Irish Times* of 19 May, 2000.

'I often think about teachers and nurses. They must be robbing banks on the side.'

You could call it the luck of the Irish – except in recent years, most young Irish have been anything but lucky in the housing market. Dublin is already one of the most expensive cities for housing in Europe – outpacing Amsterdam, the Netherlands; Brussels, Belgium; Madrid, Spain; and Rome – and prices are expected to rise another 20 percent in the next year.

The skyrocketing prices are fueled by Ireland's roaring economy, which has grown more than 8 percent in each of the last five years. That growth rate is higher than any country in the European Union, and the Organization for Economic Cooperation and Development reported this spring that Irish wealth per person is now greater than that of the U.K.

Much of the success is due to a high-tech boom. One-third of all PCs sold in Europe are made in Ireland. Nineteen of the top 25 computer and software companies in the world have set up shop in the country. Ireland also has a booming domestic industry that has produced Nasdaq darlings such as internet security firm Baltimore Technologies and Iona Technologies, which provides software for Web-based portals.

But the boom, known as the Celtic Tiger, also has its price. Ireland's thriving economy has brought more higher-paying jobs to the country, but it has also produced traffic jams, inflation and a frenetic pace of life that many find unpalatable. Dublin has, in effect, become the San Francisco of Europe.

Take traffic: 'It's official. Traffic in Dublin city center moves at the average speed the horse and cart did about 100 years ago,' says Emily-Jane Homan, who runs a small communications company in Dublin.

She's almost right. Since 1996, 321,000 cars have been added to Dublin's roads – 100,000 this year alone. Plummeting unemployment has only made the situation worse. Today, there are twice as many commuters as there were in 1991. The result: The average speed during morning rush hour is about 12 kilometers per hour, or about 7.5 miles per hour.

Although there are plans to build out the light-rail system, widen roads and create cycling lanes, the traffic isn't likely to improve any time soon. 'The trouble with such sudden growth is that it isn't easy to respond to in a short timeframe,' says John Henry, director at the Dublin Transportation Office.

While the pace of traffic has ground almost to a halt, the pace of daily life has sped up dramatically. Gone are the days when young Irish wandered on foot to their local pubs. In the new Dublin, chic restaurants are plentiful – and always booked far in advance.

'The pace is frenetic,' Homan says. 'You have to plan all your activities well in advance so that you'll be sure to get a table in a restaurant, parking in town and be able to get home.'

There is little the government, or anyone else, can do to ease the pain of development. Economists and government ministers say macro issues such as rising inflation and a potential labor shortage could throw the economy off the rails entirely.

Unemployment is down to an 18-year low of 4.6 percent, but inflation surged last month to 5.3 percent, a rate that threatens to destroy the wage restraint that has underpinned Ireland's economic success. The European union commissioner for economic and monetary affairs, Pedro Solbes, has warned that the Irish economy risks overheating, and has urged the government to use fiscal and other measures to slow the rate of growth.

'This is a classic case of demand outstripping supply,' says Daniel McCoy, an economist at Dublin's Economic and Social Research Institute. 'We are trapped in a virtuous circle. The big tech companies came to Dublin because of the tax breaks. The young people came because there was more money and jobs. With more money, they bought more cars and more houses. The problem is, the demand kept coming.'

Still, no one talks about going back to the good old days. 'There were only bad old days,' ISI's Ryan says. 'I don't know what I would do if the boom weren't going on. I graduated with a degree in art. Life's not all rosy, but it's definitely better.'

8 *infamous* ['ɪnfəməs]: well known for being bad or evil **18** *on the side* (infml): in addition to your main job **19** *the luck of the Irish:* reference to the proverbial attribute of Irish people of always having good luck **21** *anything but:* not at all **23** *outpace sb./sth.:* go, rise, improve, etc. faster than sth./sb. **28** *skyrocketing* (adj): rising extremely fast **28** *fuel sth.:* be the driving force behind sth. **32–33** *Organization for Economic Cooperation and Development (OECD):* international organization founded in 1961 to further the economic development of the European countries, Japan, Canada and the USA **40** *set up shop* (infml): establish a business or part of a business **42** *Nasdaq:* US electronic stock exchange (= Börse) which deals with, among other things, technology stocks (= Aktien) **42** *darling* (n) (infml): here, favoured company for investors **50** *frenetic:* involving a lot of energy and activity that is not organized **50** *pace:* Tempo **51** *unpalatable* [ʌn'pælətəbl]: ungenießbar **54–55** *horse and cart:* Pferdewagen **60** *plummet* (v): fall suddenly and quickly from a high position **67** *light-rail system:* system of local or short-distance train service **73–74** *grind to a halt:* slow down gradually and then stop completely **87** *labor* (AE) = (BE) *labour shortage:* lack of workers **87** *throw sth. off the rails:* bring sth. into disorder **90** *surge:* suddenly increase **92** *wage restraint:* Lohnzurückhaltung **92** *underpin sth.:* support sth. **97** *fiscal* (adj): relating to taxes **99** *demand* (n): (im Handel) Nachfrage **99** *outstrip sb./sth.:* become larger, more important, etc. than sb./sth. **100** *supply* (n): (im Handel) Angebot **102** *virtuous circle:* reference to a 'vicious circle' (= Teufelskreis), here the self-repeating events are positive or desirable **104** *tax break:* special advantage or reduction in taxes **113** *rosy* (infml): good, successful

Ireland's poorhouse image is gone – but will prosperity last?

1. According to the text, what is the economic situation in Ireland and how did it get that way?
2. Look at the adjectives and expressions which the writer uses in her assessment of the economy (cf. ll. 28–98). What do they have in common? What is their general effect?
3. What role does time play in Ireland's booming economy? How does it affect people's everyday lives?
4. In ll. 17–18 it is suggested that nurses earn less than people in the computer and media industries, for example. Explain and comment on this imbalance.
5. Look at the cartoon on pp. 18–19. How would you interpret the cartoonist's view of the 'Celtic Tiger'? What or who do the gladiators and the people beneath the Tiger represent?

The pace of life is quickening in Ireland's growing capital.

The Tiger Economy

The phenomenal level of economic growth in Ireland since the 1980s is unequalled in the Western world. The extent of the Irish 'economic miracle' can be seen in the table below, which shows the development of Ireland's Gross Domestic Product (GDP) – the total value of all goods and services produced in one year – and the GDP per capita over a period of six recent years.

	1996	1997	1998	1999	2000	2001
GDP*	58,059	67,017	77,569	89,770	102,920	114,480
GDP** per capita	16,011	18,306	20,936	23,971	27,175	29,820

*in million Euros **in Euros Source: Central Statistics Office of Ireland

When seen in a larger historical perspective, Ireland's economic transformation is even more stunning. Northern Europe's historical land of poverty, hardship and emigration was the continent's fastest growing economy in the 1990s and first years of the millenium. As a result Ireland has become an attractive place to live, both for native Irish, a lot of whom previously left or would have left in search of jobs elsewhere, and for many immigrants who have made their home there. And the rural idyll that the famous Irish politician Eamon de Valera dreamed of in the 1940s has given way to a modern society with social patterns that appear much like those of other Western countries.

Above: high-tech industry has arrived. Below: a memorial to famine victims against the background of Dublin's new prosperity.

The birth of the Tiger

The reasons for Ireland's economic boom are summed up in the following five points:

- *Capital investment:* Ireland has managed to attract huge investment of capital by mainly US corporations looking for a profitable base from which to service the lucrative European market. This development has been mainly in the sectors of computers, pharmaceuticals and health care (cf. Text 1 in this chapter). With the large number of foreign companies located there, author Fintan O'Toole has called Ireland the 'most globalised economy in the world'.
- *Tax incentives:* Foreign capital is drawn to Ireland primarily by the attractively low taxes in certain sectors. The Irish government's tax rate on corporate profits is only 12.5% (Germany's tax rate, among the lowest in the EU, is 25%).
- *New service sectors:* US firms doing business in Ireland, their numbers by far the highest in Europe, are not a threat to most smaller Irish manufacturers. On the contrary, many medium-sized Irish businesses have profited from the presence of those companies by selling them various goods and services.
- *EU membership:* The European Union has provided Ireland with some key impulses, including access to a huge market, millions of Euros in development funding from the EU's Cohesion and Structural Funds, and substantial subsidies for Irish farmers to bridge the gap between world market prices and high production costs. However, the love affair between Ireland and Europe has been dampened in recent years by EU criticism of Ireland's large budget deficit, which

goes against the EU's anti-inflation programme, and by Irish voters' initial rejection of the Nice Treaty (cf. Text 2 in this chapter), which signalled their dissatisfaction with, among other things, the higher financial burden due to the eastward expansion of the EU and the dominating role of the Union's larger states (France, Germany and the UK).

- *Domestic factors:* Certain factors at home have greatly contributed to the economic miracle. First, there is a general and stable pro-business political climate in Ireland which is watched over by the major parties, mainly by the long-ruling Fianna Fáil. Second, the country offers foreign investors a young, English-speaking and well-educated workforce (uniquely, a high proportion of the working population is composed of the younger, more productive age groups; also, for decades the government has invested much money in education, especially vocational training). Finally, labour costs are lower than in many other European countries.

How long can it last?

From a purely economic point of view, continued development in Ireland is under threat. Growth in Ireland, as in the rest of the world, has slowed down considerably. In both 2001 and 2002 the rates of growth were lower than in previous years (5.9% and 4.7%, respectively), and the Department of Finance has projected a further decline (3.5%) for 2003. The most negative by-product of the boom has been inflation. In 2002 Ireland headed the list of high-inflation countries in Europe with an inflation rate of 4.7%. A further limitation will be the reduction of the generous farming subsidies as they get shared among more EU member countries and, even more than this, as the EU reforms its Common Agricultural Policy (CAP). Nevertheless, Ireland continues to grow faster than the continental economies, and its unemployment rate is still among the lowest in the EU. At the same time, its public deficit is growing again due to excessive public spending by the government.

New problems and crony capitalism

As one might expect, there are downsides to Ireland's new prosperity. The first text in this chapter mentions the problems of housing prices, poor public transport infrastructure and a faster pace of life. The figures on the development of the Gross Domestic Product (cf. the table, p. 22) give only a hint of the growing economic inequalities in Irish society. Homelessness and poverty are still visible on Irish streets, mainly in the booming capital. In 2000 there were approx. 300 people 'sleeping rough' in Dublin (in 1969, approx. 20). It is estimated that 1250 young people under the age of 18 are homeless, most of them sleeping in subsidized hotels or similar accommodations. Moreover, the new Irish wealth is mostly concentrated in the Dublin area while some regions, especially in the North-West, are still relatively stagnant (cf. Text 3 in this chapter).

The new wealth (of some) and the accompanying free-market focus on individualism have already created a crisis of values that were traditionally thought to be 'typically Irish'. An example is the new spirit of materialism. There is also a history of widespread in corruption in Irish public life ('jobs for the boys') which goes beyond the level of such scandalous phenomena in other Western countries. However, in recent years numerous public tribunals have investigated the web of financial connections between large enterprises and Irish decision-makers in high government positions. It is already clear that some political decisions have been influenced by donations from members of the economic elite. Common features of this 'crony capitalism' are: refined strategies to avoid paying taxes; the manipulation of public planning processes to favour builders and property developers; and the payment of 'credits' to export businesses in order to protect them against non-payment in high-profit but risky foreign trade.

A contribution to peace?

A more positive influence is the important role which Ireland's strong economy can play in political developments in Northern Ireland. Economic prosperity and the pragmatism of Irish life could be having a gradual cooling effect on the sectarian fanaticisms that underlie the Troubles in the North. Growth, more jobs and better living standards may help ease tensions between Protestants and Catholics, as Protestants are persuaded to let go of their traditional view of the Irish Republic as a priest-ridden, economically impotent and chronically poor part of Ireland.

2 Ireland Goes Europe? John Ardagh

In a controversial referendum in June 2001 the Irish people voted 'no' to the Treaty of Nice, which would introduce structural changes in the European Union in preparation for a larger Union with more member states. In a second referendum in October 2002 the treaty was finally accepted. A look at the history of Ireland's relations with Europe is useful in putting these results into perspective.

'So you come from *Europe*!' said an elderly Dublin lady to my German wife, as if it were another planet. Closely involved with Britain for so long, then with the United States, the Irish had long tended to ignore the Continent. But then came the European Community, which has been a success for Ireland; through it, the Irish have slowly been developing new links, human and cultural as well as economic, with this strange planet Europe. [...]

'Through Europe, Ireland is achieving a new modern identity, a means of escape from its old backwardness, its parochialism and over-dependence on Britain,' says that passionate Euro-idealist, Professor Richard Kearney. He and others stress that Ireland did have its own early links with the Continent, before it was an English colony. They point to the sixth- to eighth-century missionaries who left 'the island of saints and scholars' to spread culture and Christianity. Then in the sixteenth to eighteenth centuries many Irish fled to the Catholic countries of Europe to escape persecution at home; Irish seminaries were set up there; Irish soldiers fought in the armies of France, Spain and Austria; more recently, Joyce chose Paris for his voluntary exile, and Beckett too, who even wrote in French. But, compared to the bear-hug of England, did these links really add up to much? From the ending of the anti-Catholic laws in 1829, up until the 1970s, this 'offshore island of an offshore island' remained peripheral to the culture and way of life of the Continent, starved of its richness; as Patrick Kavanagh wrote in his poem *Lough Derg* in the 1940s, it was 'all Ireland that froze for want of Europe.'

Garret FitzGerald, Ireland's architect of EC integration

The Common Market then produced the thaw. The Irish saw what benefits it could bring, and in their 1972 referendum they voted 'yes' to joining, by 83 per cent. Garret FitzGerald, who became foreign minister in 1973, was the enlightened pro-European who set Ireland on the path of being an active and positive member of the Community – 'He succeeded in making London look peripheral to Europe, while Dublin was metropolitan,' wrote his friend and admirer, Roy Jenkins. Haughey then took over the same policy, even declaring in 1990, with typical Haughey hype, that the EC was 'the greatest force for good that the world has ever known'. Ireland's struggling farmers might not put it quite like that, today. But the EC (EU) has always been supported by all the main political parties, and has never proved the same divisive issue as in Britain. And Ireland has provided some excellent European leaders, notably Peter Sutherland and Ray McSharry as Commissioners in Brussels.

The Irish have handled their six-monthly presidencies well, and are rightly proud of the reputation they have won as perhaps the most effective of smaller member States. It has brought Ireland an entirely new voice in the world.

Today the farmers and some others may be sceptical, but most people remain pro-European. The EC has helped Ireland more than most member States – in at least six specific ways. First, in economic terms, it has greatly reduced the over-dependence on the British market. Second, politically and psychologically, it has enabled the old unequal face-to-face relationship with Britain to change into a new, more relaxed partnership, within a wider club where both are equal members; and this has eased the old Irish complex about the English. Third, it has impelled Ireland to modernize socially, in certain areas: the ending of the ban on married women in the civil service, and the laws on equal pay for women, were both due to the EC. Fourth, it has obliged Ireland to improve its environmental policies. Fifth, whatever the problems today with the CAP, this farming country has benefited enormously from the EU's budgetary emphasis on agriculture. Last, Ireland through persistent lobbying has gained more from the lucrative new Structural Funds than the other poorer members: it has presented its case better than Greece or Portugal, and has gained some £7.2 billion from these funds for 1994–9. Sceptics point out that, if the EU provides them with such hand-outs, then of course the Irish are in favour of it; and some criticize the politicians for what one student called 'their non-stop begging-bowl approach – it's all take-take-take, so humiliating'. Garret FitzGerald admitted to me: 'Yes, for most people the EU *is* a matter of economic self-interest, not of idealism or emotion. The element of true idealism is small – but it's influential.'

8 *parochialism* [pə'rəʊkiəl-] (fml) (derog): only concerned with small issues that happen in your local area and not interested in more important things **14** *persecution:* cruel and unfair treatment of a person, usu. because of his/her religious or political beliefs **15** *seminary:* college where Catholic priests are trained **16** *Joyce = James Joyce* (1882–1941): Irish novelist and short-story writer; his works include the novel *Ulyssess* (1922) and the short stories *Dubliners* (1914) **17** *Beckett = Samuel Beckett* (1906–1989): Irish playwright, best known for his play *Waiting for Godot* (1953) **17** *bear-hug:* act of showing affection for sb. by holding them tightly and strongly in your arms; (here) colonial domination and later close cultural and economic ties
18–19 *anti-Catholic laws:* after the defeat of the Irish by the Protestant British at the end of the 1600s discriminatory laws ('Penal Laws') were passed against the native population of Ireland which restricted their economic possibilities and forced a tenant (= Mieter, Pächter) system on the majority
21 *starve sb./sth. of sth.:* not give sb./sth. sth. that is needed **21** *Patrick Kavanagh* (1904–1967) ['kævənə]: Irish poet, best known for his collection *The Great Hunger* (1942 **23** *thaw:* situation in which the relations between two or more unfriendly countries become more friendly **25** *Garret FitzGerald* (born 1926): Irish economist, leader of Fine Gael (Ireland's second-largest political party) 1977–1987, foreign minister 1973–1977, prime minister of Ireland 1981–1987 **30** *Charles Haughey* (born 1925) ['hɔːhi]: leader of Fianna Fáil (Ireland's largest political party) 1979–1992, prime minister of Ireland 1979–1982 and 1987–1992; he was later found to be involved in corruption scandals during his time in office **52** *oblige sb. to do sth.* [ə'blaɪdʒ]: force sb. to do sth, by law, because it is a duty, etc. **53** *CAP* (abbr) = *Common Agricultural Policy:* (in der EU) Gemeinsame Agrarpolitik **60–61** *begging-bowl approach:* practice of asking others for money **61** *humiliating* (adj): demütigend

Ireland has become a strong partner in European affairs.

1. Sum up the writer's view of the role the European continent played in the course of Irish history.
2. Describe the political cartoon on p. 26 and explain its message based on the information in the text.
3. Using keywords, summarize the ways in which the EC/EU has helped Ireland (cf. ll. 43–58 and the Info, p.22).
4. Irish voters rejected the Nice Treaty in June 2001 (cf. the introduction) by a margin of 54% to 46%. In the October 2002 referendum voters said 'yes' to the treaty by a margin of 63% to 37%. What possible reasons does the text offer for either of these decisions?
5. Imagine the German people were asked to give their opinion about the Nice Treaty. Find out about the Treaty, then speculate on the result of a German referendum. Give reasons for your view.

3 The Tiger Vincent Byrne

The fanciful term 'Celtic Tiger' has turned out to be very useful for promotional purposes and has, of course, lent itself to many comments by cartoonists, critics and others. It also inspired Vincent Byrne, a member of the Dublin Writers Workshop to pen the following poem expressing his view of Ireland's economic reality.

Its growl was heard once in Kenmare
but it was never seen.
They tought they'd found its prints in Clare
where it had never been.
A fur ball found in Sligo town
they claim came from its throat,
but some suspect a local's cat
for it wears the same striped coat.

And a postman down in Skibbereen
swears it leapt on him one night,
as from the pub he staggered home
but the beast it didn't bite,
just licked him over like a stamp
and stuck him to the ground,
where in the morning fast asleep
the postman he was found.

But I know well these stories,
sure they cannot be but lies,
for the creature seldom leaves the Pale
and when it does it flies.
It lives a life of luxury
surrounded by its pals,
the other fat cats of this Isle
the other likely lads.
It's never seen a field of hay,
It cannot milk a cow,
It doesn't know the price of bread
or the purpose of a plough.
It knows that fish swim in the sea
and are caught in great big nets,
but it's not surprised the dopes get snagged
for none it's seen have heads.

I hope that this wee beastie
realises pretty quick
that all its fun and frolicking
could make it pretty sick.
If it doesn't come to grips real fast
with the debt it owes to us
and start to share its wealth around
this patronising puss
will find itself back in the zoo
on valium and prozac
a wasted opportunist,
a crippled Celtic cat.

1 *Kenmare:* town in County Kerry (cf. map, inside cover) **3** *Clare:* county in western Ireland (cf. map, inside cover) **5** *fur ball:* Knäuel von Haaren, die Katzen beim Putzen verschlucken und später wieder erbrechen **5** *Sligo:* town in County Sligo, north-western Ireland **7** *local* (n): person who lives in a particular place or district **9** *Skibbereen:* town in County Cork, (cf. map, inside cover) **19** *Pale:* historical region round Dublin **22** *pal* (infml): friend **23** *fat cat* (infml) (derog): person who earns or has a lot of money **24** *likely lad* (infml): young man who shows the potential to be successful in business **28** *plough* [plaʊ]: Pflug **31** *dope* (derog): stupid person (here, animal) **31** *get snagged:* be caught **33** *wee* (infml): very small in size **33** *beastie* (infml): diminutive form of beast; animal, esp. one that is large, dangerous or unusual **35** *frolick* [ˈfrɒlɪk ☆ ˈfrɑː-]: herumtollen **37–38** *come to grips with sth.:* begin to understand and deal with sth. difficult **40** *patronising* [ˈpætrə- ☆ ˈpeɪ-] (adj) (derog): showing that you feel better or more intelligent than sb. else **40** *puss* [pʊs] (infml): Katze, Mieze **42** *valium and prozac:* two types of drugs which are used as sedatives **43** *wasted* (adj) (sl): strongly affected by alcohol or drugs

1. Who is the speaker, or who does he or she represent? Explain your answer, using examples from the text.
2. What is the speaker's basic message?
3. Describe the tone of the poem. Illustrate your answer with examples from the text.
4. The poet uses various rhetorical devices in the poem. Find examples of alliteration, assonance and consonance and describe their function.
5. Look at the cartoon on p. 28. What do you think the cartoonist is trying to say by presenting 'Paddy' and 'Kathleen' in this way?
6. Write a short poem whose tone mirrors that of Byrne's poem. The title: 'The Tiger's Answer'.

Emigrants of Old, Immigrants of New

1 Exiles Patrick Hennessy

There are few Irish families that have not experienced emigration at some time in their history. The Irish artist Patrick Hennessy pictorialised his own perspective on Irish emigration in this painting from 1943.

1. What is your reaction to Hennessy's painting? Try to describe it in no more than three words. Discuss your ideas.
2. Describe what you see in the painting.
3. What sort of mood or atmosphere does Hennessy create? Make a list of elements which contribute to this effect.
4. Look at the perspective from which the scene is viewed. Why do you think the artist chose this perspective?
5. Study the information in the graph below and discuss how it relates to the painting.
6. Compare the experience which is depicted in the painting with similar experiences of people elsewhere in the world in recent times.

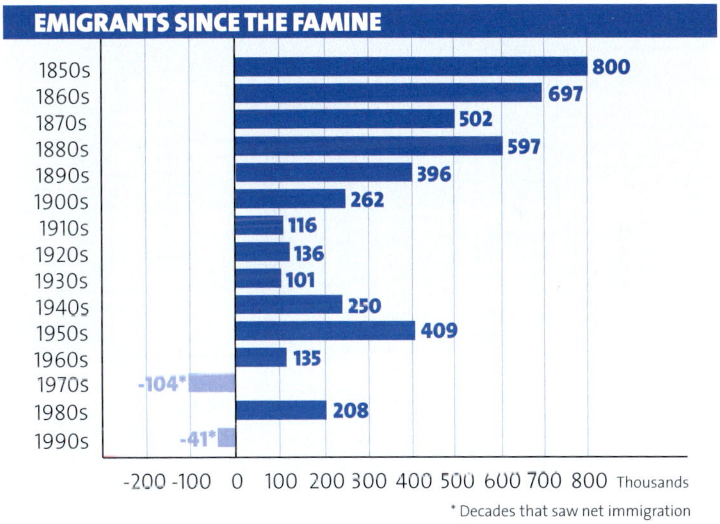

(Source: CSO and Paul Sweeney *The Celtic Tiger – Ireland's Economic Miracle Explained*)

2 We'll Be Together in America Someday

Frank McCourt

In this excerpt from his partly fictionalized autobiography *Angela's Ashes* (1996) Irish-American author Frank McCourt describes his last days at home in the town of Limerick before leaving Ireland to look for work. The time is the late 1940s and Frank is 19 years old.

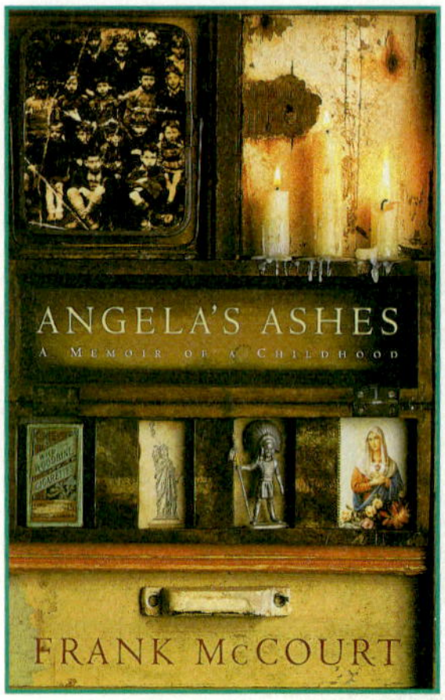

Limerick in the 1940s; Michael Legge (inset, right) as young Frank McCourt in the film version of Angela's Ashes (1999).

I tell Mam I'm going in a few weeks and she cries. Michael says, Will we all go some day?

We will.

Alphie says, Will you send me a cowboy hat and a thing you throw that comes back to you?

Michael tells him that's a boomerang and you'd have to go all the way to Australia to get the likes of that, you can't get it in America.

Alphie says you can get it in America yes you can and they argue about America and Australia and boomerangs till Mam says, For the love o' Jesus, yeer brother is leaving us and the two of ye are there squabbling over boomerangs. Will ye give over?

Mam says we'll have to have a bit of party the night before I go. They used to have parties in the old days when anyone would go to America, which was so far away the parties were called American wakes because the family never expected to see the departing one again in this life. She says 'tis a great pity Malachy can't come back from England but we'll be together in America someday with the help of God and His Blessed Mother.

On my days off from work I walk around Limerick and look at all the places we lived, the Windmill Street, Hartstonge Street, Roden Lane, Rosbrien Road, Little Barrington Street, which is really a lane. I stand looking at Theresa Carmody's house till her mother comes out and says, What do you want? I sit at the graves of Oliver and Eugene in the old St. Patrick's Burying Ground and cross the road to St. Lawrence's Cemetery where Theresa is buried. Wherever I go I hear voices of the dead and I wonder if they can follow you across the Atlantic Ocean.

I want to get pictures of Limerick stuck in my head in case I never come back. I sit in St. Joseph's Church and the Redemptorist church and tell myself take a good look because I might never see this again. I walk down Henry Street to say good-bye to St. Francis though I'm sure I'll be able to talk to him in America.

Now there are days I don't want to go to America. I'd like to go to O'Riordan's Travel Agency and get back my fifty-five pounds. I could wait till I'm twenty-one and Malachy can go with me so that I'll know at least one person in New York. I have strange feelings and sometimes when I'm sitting by the fire with Mam and my brothers I feel tears coming and I'm ashamed of myself for being weak. At first Mam laughs and tells me, Your bladder must be near your eye, but then Michael says, We'll all go to America, Dad will be there, Malachy will be there and we'll all be together, and she gets the tears herself and we sit there, the four of us, like weeping eejits.

Mam says this is the first time we ever had a party and isn't it a sad thing altogether that you have it when your children are slipping away one by one, Malachy to England, Frank to America. She saves a few shillings from her wages taking care of Mr. Sliney to buy bread, ham, brawn, cheese, lemonade and a few bottles of stout. Uncle Pa Keating brings stout, whiskey and a little sherry for Aunt Aggie's delicate stomach and she brings a cake loaded with currants and raisins she baked herself. The Abbot brings six bottles of stout and says, That's all right, Frankie, ye can all drink it as long as I have a bottle or two for meself to help me sing me song.

He sings "The Road to Rasheen." He holds his stout, closes his eyes, and song comes out in a high whine. The words make no sense and everyone wonders why tears are seeping from his shut eyes. Alphie whispers to me, Why is he crying over a song that makes no sense?

I don't know.

The Abbot ends his song, opens his eyes, wipes his cheeks and tells us that was a sad song about an Irish boy that went to America and got shot by gangsters and died before a priest could reach his side and he tells me don't be gettin' shot if you're not near a priest.

Uncle Pa says that's the saddest song he ever heard and is there any chance we could have something lively. He calls on Mam and she says, Ah, no, Pa, sure I don't have the wind.

Come on, Angela, come on. One voice now, one voice and one voice only.

All right. I'll try.

We all join in the chorus of her sad song.

A mother's love is a blessing
No matter where you roam.
Keep her while you have her,
You'll miss her when she's gone.

Uncle Pa says one song is worse than the one before and are we turning this night into a wake altogether, is there any chance someone would sing a song to liven up the proceedings or will he be driven to drink with the sadness.

Oh, God, says Aunt Aggie, I forgot. The moon is having an eclipse abroad this minute.

We stand out in the lane watching the moon disappear behind a round black shadow. Uncle Pa says, That's a very good sign for you going to America, Frankie.

No, says Aunt Aggie, 'tis a bad sign. I read in the paper that the moon is practicing for the end of the world.

Oh, end of the world my arse, says Uncle Pa. 'Tis the beginning for Frankie McCourt. He'll come back in a few years with a new suit and fat on his bones like any Yank and a lovely girl with white teeth hangin' from his arm.

Mam says, Ah, no, Pa, ah, no, and they take her inside and comfort her with a drop of sherry from Spain.

1 *Mam* (IrE infml): mother
7 *the likes of that* (infml) something like that
9 *o'* (IrE infml): of
10 *yeer* (IrE infml): your
10 *ye* (IrE infml): you
10 *squabble over sth.:* argue noisily about sth. that is notvery important
11 *give over* (IrE infml): (in spoken language) used to tell sb. to stop doing sth. 14 *wake* (n): (in Ireland) festivities held after a funeral (= Beerdigung), usually celebrated with lots of drinking 15 *'tis* (IrE infml): it is 16 *Malachy:* (in the book) author's brother who has gone off to work in England 17 *Blessed* ['blesɪd]: gesegnet
20–21 *Theresa Carmody:* (in the book) author's first girlfriend, who is now dead 22 *Oliver, Eugene:* author's dead brothers 27 *Redemptorist church:* religious congregation founded in Italy and first established in Limerick in 1853; its main aim is to do missionary work among the poor 29 *St. Francis = St. Francis of Assisi* (?1181–1226): Italian monk and founder of the Franciscan monastic order who is highly revered by Catholics 39 *weep* (v): cry 39 *eejit* (IrE sl): idiot 42 *shilling:* former British coin used in the 1930s (also used in the Irish Free State) 43 *brawn:* (im UK und in Irland) Sülze 44 *stout:* strong dark beer 46 *The Abbot:* (in the book) nickname of a family friend 48 *me* (IrE infml): my 50 *whine* (n): long high sound that is usu. unpleasant or annoying 60 *have the wind:* genügend Atem oder Kraft haben 64 *blessing* (n): Segen 71 *eclipse:* (Mond)finsternis 78 *my arse* (IrE sl) (derog): used by some people to show that they do not believe what sb. has said (*arse* = Arsch) 80 *Yank = Yankee* (infml) (often derog): person from the USA

Author Frank McCourt (right) with his younger brother Malachy in January 2000. Both live in the USA.

1. How do the different characters deal with the final farewell situation?
2. Describe the tone of the text, using examples to support your conclusion.
3. Analyse the behaviour of the narrator's mother, Angela, in this scene. What do you think might be the meaning behind the book's title, *Angela's Ashes*?
4. Discuss some of the stylistic elements in the text and their effects.
5. What impression of America do the different characters have? What does this suggest about the situation in Ireland, or Irish people's perception of themselves, at the time?
6. Role-play: One person takes the role of Frank and others are the members and friends of his family (Mam, Uncle Pa Keating, The Abbot, Aunt Aggie, Michael, Alphie). Frank's family and friends give their reactions to his announcement that he's going to America. Prepare your arguments beforehand from your character's point of view. Afterwards, discuss as a class to what extent the characters were well represented.

From Emigration to Immigration

History of farewells

Ireland – a country of immigrants? The idea seems to go against the common image of the Emerald Isle, which for centuries has sent its people out into the world. Some historical facts:

– Between 1788 and 1868 over 50,000 Irish men, women and children were exiled as convicts to Australia;
– Early in the 19th century it was unemployment which drove tens of thousands of Irish to Scotland and England, as well as to America;
– Hunger and disease caused by the Great Potato Famine of 1845–1849 forced millions more to leave their homeland;
– The steady exodus in the years after the Famine was of similar proportions, with over four million Irish leaving between 1851 and 1921.

As the table 'Emigrants Since the Famine' (cf. p. 31) illustrates, the tide of emigration did not turn significantly until the end of the 1980s.

Top: Emigrants awaiting their departure on the quayside at Cork, ca. 1850. Bottom: New faces of Ireland.

A new trend

In recent times the demographic make-up of the Republic of Ireland has changed profoundly. Attracted by the rapidly growing economy (cf. Chapter II), many long-time Irish emigrants or their children have returned to their homeland. This influx was particularly high throughout the 1990s. In the period from 1995 to 2000 roughly a quarter of a million people migrated to Ireland. About half of them were Irish returnees. The other half of this new immigrant population came mostly from the United Kingdom (18%), other states in the European Union (13%) and the USA (7%).

Controversial newcomers

Reactions in the Irish Republic to the growing numbers of immigrants have been mixed. In the past the few immigrants, notably Italians and Chinese, were met with reserve and caution but, because of their small numbers, they were more or less accepted. This attitude was probably best explained by the country's lack of economic opportunities. The spectacular success of the economy and a drastically improved job market have created a new situation. This is reflected in the heated public debate over immigration policy. Historically, as Ireland did not draw many foreign migrants, the government gave little consideration to a formal policy towards them. Now the country is faced with the need for clearly defined immigration and integration policies.

Returning Irish and immigrants from EU and European Economic Area states have a right to live and work in Ireland. This is guaranteed by the Irish Constitution of 1937 and by EU law. While the presence of these migrants has not generated any public debate, more controversial are the three other categories of migrants: asylum-seekers (e.g. from Asian and African countries), civil-war refugees (from Kosovo, Bosnia, etc.), and highly skilled and other immigrants from non-European countries. Each of these groups must be dealt with differently, and their legal status is further complicated by international laws governing their treatment.

Defining a coherent policy

The public debate focuses largely on the question of how to deal with asylum seekers, whose numbers rose steadily during the 1990s (cf. the table below). Although the ratio of asylum seekers to the native population is far lower than, for example, in Germany, the new situation has caused concern in this country of only 3.8 million people and has led to a variety of responses from the Irish government.

The government's policy appears to make the asylum-seeking process difficult and unattractive: financial assistance has been drastically reduced, housing for refugees is limited and the right to work or to study is denied. Asylum seekers are systematically distributed around the country in order to prevent large groupings that might provoke racist attacks. Authorities have even considered placing asylum seekers on 'floating hotels' anchored in the Irish Sea. Under their deportation policy, the government offers millions of Euros to home countries in order to help speed up the relocation of deportees.

These measures are partly the result of hardening attitudes within the population towards asylum seekers. More liberal voices point to the lessons of history. Commentator Fintan O'Toole, for instance, asserts that 'the presence among us of people born in other countries brings us closer to the experience of our emigrants' and helps to establish an inclusive Irish identity based on a steady stream of coming and going. But while such internationalism and open-mindedness can be found in the columns of Ireland's leading newspaper, *The Irish Times*, it does not seem to reflect the mood of many Irish. Articles and letters to the editor in other Irish newspapers strike a different tone, expressing fear, for example, that asylum seekers might bring in diseases, and strictly denouncing 'economic migrants' (cf. this chapter, Text 4), despite Ireland's own history of poverty-fleeing emigrants. Some politicians complain about the 'floods' of asylum seekers. Racist websites and attacks on Africans and others are on the increase (cf. this chapter, Text 3). 'You'll notice the extraordinarily virulent racism that has become a feature of Irish life', says one British tourist guide. This may be exaggerated and an unfair generalisation, but racist language and behaviour have come to threaten Ireland's image as the 'land of a thousand welcomes' and its status as a caring nation.

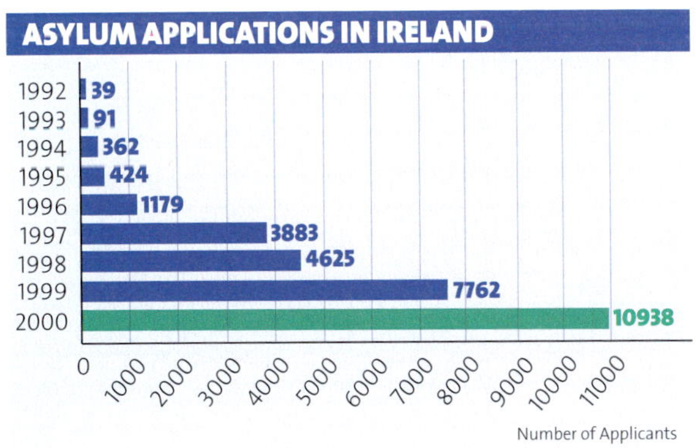

Source: Department of Justice, Equality and Law Reform, *Irish Times*, 6 January, 2000

3 The Siren's Voice Christy Moore

In Greek mythology the sirens were creatures who were part woman, part bird. With their beautiful singing they attracted men in sailing ships, who sailed toward the island on which they lived, and fell victim to the rocks and dangerous waters. The Irish folk singer Christy Moore makes use of this ancient motif in this song from 1999.

Somalia, Somalia.

She picked up a handful of earth and kisssing it, she cried;
'The song of our village has come to an end'.

Then she heard the siren's voice
And the siren's voice was singing;
Island of the welcomes. One hundred thousand welcomes.
Christian holy island. One hundred thousand welcomes.
Land of the Holy Fathers. One hundred thousand welcomes.
Land of the Saints and scholars. One hundred thousand welcomes.

Ancient city of the deep lagoon. Céad míle fáilte.
Heart of The Rowl. Céad míle fáilte.
Dublin city of the rare auld times. Céad míle fáilte.
Where the green snot river flows. Céad míle fáilte.

Again she heard the siren's voice
And the siren's voice was singing;
Black life, white life, pro-life,
Black life, white life, pro-life,
Black lies, white lies, no life.

Again she heard the siren's voice
And the siren's voice was singing;
No niggers or knackers or wogs, no refugees.
No Día is Muire, sez she,
And no divorce in Heaven, sez she, no refugees.
Céad míle fáilte.
A míle fáilte my arse, sez she.
Míle fáilte my arse.

1. How do the first three lines relate to the rest of the song?
2. What is the siren's role?
3. Which stereotypes about immigrants and refugees does Christy Moore refer to (cf. also Info, p. 36)?
4. How does Christy Moore comment on the controversy going on in Irish society?

Living off our land,
Living off our land,
Living off our hard-earned surplus,
Creating housing shortages and unemployment.
Living off our land.
They're coming here to save us,
Saving the white babies.
They're coming here to save us,
Saving white babies souls.
The siren's voice was heard.

3 *siren* ['saɪrən] **9** *city of the deep lagoon:* ancient name for Dublin (from the Gaelic word *dubhlinn* = dark pool) **9** *céad míle fáilte* [ˌkeɪd ˌmiːlə 'fɔːltʃə] (Gaelic): a hundred thousand welcomes; traditional Irish greeting that is widely used by the tourist industry **10** *Heart of the Rowl* (IrE sl): the best; the expression is used in the popular Irish folk song 'Dicey Reilly' to describe the hard-drinking Dublin woman of the same name **11** *auld* [ɔːld] (Gaelic): old **12** *snot* (n) (infml): Rotz **20** *nigger* (sl) (derog): black person **20** *knacker* ['nækə] (IrE sl) (derog): Zigeuner (in Irland „traveller" genannt) **20** *wog* (IrE sl) (derog): foreigner, esp. one who is not white **21** *Día is Muire* ['diːə ɪs 'mɪː] (Gaelic): God and Mary; traditional Irish form of reply to 'Dia duit' (= God to you) **21** *sez* (infml): says **24** *my arse* (IrE sl) (derog): used by some people to show that they do not believe what has been said (*arse* = Arsch) **28** *surplus:* (here) profit

4 Welcome to Ireland
Andy Pollock, Derek Speirs

In recent years Ireland has been a destination for people fleeing war, economic hardship and political persecution. The following stories are taken from the book *A Part of Ireland Now* (1997). They describe two rather different experiences of refugees who came to the Irish Republic to rebuild their lives.

Mr Luyindula and Mrs Bikembo

The Zairean couple, above, feel uncomfortable on Dublin's streets.

Mr Luyindula was a journalist on one of the main daily papers in the Zairean capital, Kinshasa. His 'crime' was to write a number of articles critical of the regime of the then dictator, President Mobutu. He was arrested and thrown into jail. What saved him was that he became seriously ill and had to be transferred to a hospital for an operation. While there his family, colleagues and the opposition movement of which he was a member arranged his escape by dug-out canoe across the Congo river to Brazzaville, the capital of the neighbouring Republic of Congo.

He was put on a plane, beside a Congolese businessman who was travelling to Ireland, and flown to Dublin. He found himself, with only a few words of English and very little money, in the centre of a strange European city.

Eventually he found the offices of the Irish Refugee Council and they helped him to apply for political asylum at the Department of Justice.

Back in Kinshasa, Mrs Bikembo had moved out of her home with their two children before the police arrived. Finding her gone, they arrested his younger brother instead. But knowing they were still looking for her, she started to make arrangements to join her husband in Ireland. She arrived in May 1996, a few months before he was granted asylum.

They are currently going through the procedures to have their two children – who are still with their grandparents in Kinshasa – join them under the UN's family reunification programme.

Mr Luyindula was lucky to get a flat in north Dublin from another refugee who was being repatriated. He is now studying English and computers at a FAS centre in Baldoyle, while his wife learns English at a city centre college.

But apart from that, their experience of Ireland has not been a happy one. Two years ago he was beaten up by a group of youths in broad daylight in a street in Temple Bar, with passers-by failing to intervene to help him.

They received an anonymous racist hate letter sent to 'The African' at their new flat. Both Catholics, they attend the local church every Sunday. Recently a man started insulting Mrs Bikembo in the middle of Mass, and she had to be rescued by concerned parishioners. They have lost count of the times people in the street have told them to go back to Africa.

'When I came here everybody seemed friendly, saying 'Hello' and greeting me in the street. I was grateful that Ireland had taken me in when I was in danger in my own country,' says Mr Luyindula. 'But since the attack I have started to see Irish people in a new light. Many of them think it's all right to have one or two black people living in Ireland. However more than that irritates them. Older people are usually nice, but younger people are often nasty, and become particularly aggressive when they are drunk.'

'I don't feel comfortable here,' says Mrs Bikembo. 'Although we are free, we feel like prisoners. I am afraid to walk in the street by myself now and my husband doesn't go out at night. The kind of racism we have experienced here does not exist in Zaire. There all foreigners, European and African, are made to feel welcome and are offered hospitality.'

Fardus Sultan

An American woman smuggled Fardus out of Sarajevo by giving her a false passport and pretending she was her secretary.

Six months earlier her parents had been among the first Bosnians to arrive in Ireland from a refugee camp in Austria. Because Sarajevo was surrounded and under daily siege, she could not immediately follow them.

In October 1993 she entered UCD to study politics and Arabic. She says the studying helped her to settle down, keep busy and make friends, although she was living in constant fear about what might happen to her fiancé – now her husband – a soldier in the Bosnian army, and other members of her family left behind in Sarajevo.

Fardus says the 'friendliness and warmth' of the people she met was a great support to her during those difficult early years. She graduated in the summer of 1996, but found it hard to get work for a year. However, in September she began working as a translator and interpreter for a Dublin firm. Her husband, who did not speak a word of English when he arrived here last year, now works as a draughtsman for Iarnrod Eireann.

Her parents have found it more difficult to adjust. Her stepfather, who owned a grocery shop in

Fardus Sultan, right, has found a new life.

Sarajevo, now works on a building site. Her mother, a lawyer in Bosnia, cannot find work here.

Fardus worries about the bad publicity surrounding Bosnian refugees in recent months and whether being Bosnian was a reason it took her so long to get a job. She says: 'There are good and bad people everywhere – you can't judge a person on the basis of nationality. No one wants to be a refugee. No one wants to leave a good life behind and start a new life in a strange, faraway country. We Bosnians are a proud people. Even if we don't have enough, we won't beg. We want to work, to make a contribution to this country, to pay our taxes.'

'I feel so much part of Ireland now. I couldn't go back to Bosnia, there's nothing for me there,' she says. 'I'm only 23 but I've already had two lives: one before the war – the innocent normal life of a teenager – and one since. I had to leave everything behind and forget my first life and adjust to Ireland. I couldn't keep asking myself what had happened during the war in Bosnia: there was no logical answer to why thousands of people's lives were destroyed just because they were of a different nationality – you'd go crazy thinking about that. To go back to Bosnia now I would have to start a third life. I wouldn't be able to take that.

Anyway I want to stay in Ireland. I feel that Ireland has given me more than my own country – it didn't have to do that for me. That's why it's so important to me that people here have a good impression of Bosnians. Because I will always carry my nationality with me. I feel in a way like a Gaelic Bosnian.'

10 *dug-out canoe:* canoe made out of log (= Baumstamm) **54** *refugee camp* [ˌrefju'dʒiː]: Flüchtlingslager **55** *under siege* [siːdʒ]: surrounded by an army or the police with no way to escape **56** *UCD* (abbr) = *University College Dublin* **58** *fiancé* [fi'ɒnseɪ ☆ ˌfiːaːn'seɪ]: *Verlobter* **62** *graduate* (v): successfully complete a university or college course **73** *Iarnrod Eireann* [ˌl̥ɪrnrɑːd 'eron]: Irish equivalent of the Deutsche Bahn

1. What made Mr Luyindula change his opinion about living in Ireland (cf. ll. 32–38)?
2. Describe Fardus's experience in her first few years in Ireland and how she feels today.
3. How would you explain the fact that the experiences of Mr Luyindula and Mrs Bikembo on the one hand and Fardus Sultan on the other are so different?
4. Mrs Bikembo says that in Zaire 'all foreigners, European and African, are made to feel welcome and are offered hospitality' (ll. 49–50). To what extent might a statement such as this one be problematic?
5. Imagine you are a political refugee living in Germany. Describe your experiences with Germans and Germany in a letter to a friend in your home country. It might help to imagine the specific country which you come from (e.g. Zaire, Cuba, or China).

5 An Open and Caring Society?

An ongoing debate in Ireland has centred around the question of whether foreigners seeking asylum here should be welcomed more, given Ireland's own history of emigration, or whether these people are a burden to the Irish social system and should thus be turned away. The following letters to the editor appeared in the *Irish Times* in May 2000.

SIR, – I'm sick of this one-sided debate on the refugee/asylum-seekers problem. The liberal left seem to think they have the moral right to impose on us, the inhabitants of this island, their interpretation of what is right or wrong.

In a democracy everybody has an equal say in how the society should be run, regardless of whether they like or don't like refugees/asylum-seekers. I'm tired of the politically correct, liberal-left finger-pointing, using the word 'racist' for anybody who disagrees with them. These people remind me of the hysterical, fanatic Catholics during the Inquisition who shouted 'heretic' as they burned innocent people at the stake.

My experience of refugees/asylum-seekers is that they are perfectly healthy, well educated, clothed in designer wear, tote mobil phones and drive cars. Perfect model citizens, exept they are funded by the hard-pressed Irish taxpayer.

So enough of this rubbish about political/religious/ethnic persecution; these people are economic migrants, pure and simple. I don't expect to be published as your paper does not take a open view on this issue. It prefers the liberal-left, politically correct view. – Yours, etc.,

DEREK GARTLAND, NAAS, CO KILDARE.

SIR, – Some asylum-seekers, and I know of a few, have received unexpected and tragic news from home since their arrival here in Ireland. At times, little more than brief messages bring the dreadful news of the death of a close relative or friend.

Today in Ireland, quiet tears are being shed by many lonely and frightened people who find themselves able to do little more than silently commune with the faces, memories and fading photographs of loved ones, whose passing is the cause of much hidden pain and sadness.

More often than not, bright faces and gentle manners mask hearts that are heavy and trauma that goes untold and unrecognised. How many more asylum-seekers grieve inwardly as they grapple with displacement, the ever-dawning reality of separation from both home and kin?

That Irish people have to be 'educated' to understand that asylum-seekers are human beings is surely our greatest indictment to date. If being Irish ever meant anything, it has surely never meant pushing people to the point of breaking, reducing people to the point of despair and being crushed.

This particular chapter of Irish history runs the risk of being our most shameful yet. To my mind at least, the powers-that-be and the mob are seeking to shape policy with too great a reference to politics, self-interest and expediency, and too grudging a regard for justice, openness or care.

As some asylum-seeker sleeps uneasily in our country tonight, I feel ashamed and diminished by what I have, up to now, been willing to tolerate from my Government, from some of my fellow countrymen and women, and even at times from myself.

To you, my brothers and sisters who have come to my country, I unreservedly offer my abject apology. I humbly ask that you bear with us, as we seek to show you what we can and ought to have already done better.

Of my fellow Irish sisters and brothers I ask for a change of heart and mind. Together let us now resolve to do as much as basic justice would require and more, as much for our own dignity as for the dignity of those we are collectively called to serve. – Yours, etc.,

FR JOHN CARROLL, ST AIDAN'S CATHEDRAL, ENNISCORTHY, CO WEXFORD.

2–3 *impose sth. on sb.:* make sb. accept sth. (esp. the same opinions, wishes, etc. as your own) **12** *tote sth.* (infml): carry sth. **13–14** *hard-pressed* (adj): having a lot of problems, esp. too much work and too little time or money **15** *persecution:* Verfolgung **26** *commune with. sb./sth.* [kə'mjuːn] (fml): share your thoughts and feelings with sb./sth. without speaking **30** *grapple with sth.:* try hard to deal with sth., esp. a difficult problem **33** *indictment* [ɪn'daɪtmənt]: sign that a system, society, etc. is very bad or wrong
39 *expediency* [ɪk'spiːdiənsi]: what is useful or necessary to do in a particular situation, but not always fair or right **39** *grudging* ['ɡrʌdʒ-] (adj): done unwillingly **45** *abject* (fml): without any pride or respect for yourself

Dublin residents show their opposition to racism and the government's handling of aslyum-seekers.

1. Summarize Derek Gartland's opinion in about 50 words.

2. According to Father John Carroll, what is hidden behind most asylum-seekers' 'bright faces and gentle manners' (l. 28)?

3. What is your reaction to Gartland's comparison of 'the liberal left' (l. 2) with 'hysterical, fanatical Catholics during the Inquisition' (l. 9)? Explain.

4. If Derek Gartland and John Carroll were to talk face-to-face about refugees and asylum-seekers, what do you think they would say to each other? Write a dialogue between the two men.

5. To what extent is a similar debate taking place in your own country? Collect information from the Internet or other sources to support your answer.

6 'They Called Her Nigger' Kathy Sheridan

Acceptance and integration are never-ending subjects for many people of colour who live in Ireland, no matter how long they have been there. The following is part of an article from the *Irish Times* of June 17, 2000.

The pretty 22-year old sits across the table in her comfortable home and describes what growing up in south Co Dublin was like: 'The number of times I was called a Paki, a nigger, a mongrel, a mixed breed ...' Her mother's eyes flicker. The daughter continues, with a wry laugh: 'Well, I know for a fact that I'm not from Pakistan. And I'm definitely not a nigger.'

Her mother looks dazed. 'They call you nigger ...' she says slowly. 'You never told me that.' Several times over the next few hours, Dr Mary Toomey would repeat those words, disbelievingly: 'They called her nigger ... she never told me that.'

To a populace still reeling at the implications of a near-fatal attack on the (white) father of a mixed-race family in Dublin's Pearse Street last weekend, it's hardly startling stuff. Aoife Toomey has no obvious wounds to show for being the child of a mixed-race marriage. No one has stabbed her, or stood outside her home yelling abuse or urinated through her letterbox.

She is a relaxed, stylish young woman who will shortly have a Trinity politics degree to add to her good fortune as the cherished only child of professional, middle-class parents. In a few weeks, she will marry Matthew, a white, all-American boy, and they will settle in the US.

The wounds only show when she mentions the children she hopes to have: 'Everyone thinks I'll come back, but I will not. I'm getting ready to start my life 3,000 miles away in a place where I don't stand out at all. I refuse to feel ashamed of being Eurasian. Here, I am expected to apologise for it, to be thankful and humble and less visible. So I will not bring children up in this place. I'm not whingeing. That's just the way it is.'

The wounds run deep. Casual abuse and naked contempt at personal and official levels have marked the long, slow erosion of dignity and identity. Now, the pain and sense of betrayal are manifest in Mary Toomey. A woman of presence and accomplishment, she married Barry Toomey, an Irish engineer, against the will of her parents, high-caste Tamils in what is now Sri Lanka. Later, she would ring with good news (another book commission), but to add: 'All afternoon, I have heard my mother's voice – "You are forgetting ... You are selfish ... My grandchildren will not belong anywhere". I now see that she was right.'

Aoife and Mary Toomey

Mary Toomey came to Ireland in 1967 to do a PhD in ecology at Trinity College. 'I brought educational assets into this country. The natural sciences were virtually unknown here and biology was being introduced in the schools, so the Department of Education had me teaching teachers from Louth to Kerry.'

In a Co Wexford village after Mass on St Patrick's Day in 1968, she was inundated with lunch invitations. 'They wanted to touch me and I remember joking: "I'm afraid I cannot part with this tan". I never once felt uncomfortable.'

She was commissioned to write the first biology text books for schools; was headhunted to work at universities; was offered a job by UNESCO (the UN's education and science organisation), to travel across the world, to talk about science education. 'I turned it down. I chose to live in Ireland because I loved it ...'

She is fiercely proud of her Tamil heritage. 'We have frescos, culture, carvings, going back to the 5th century BC. In 1963, 90 per cent of the Sri Lankan population were literate and education was prized as the jewel, through every caste. Fourteen per cent of the budget was allocated to education, which was free right through from primary to university.'

It's not a boast, just a pointed reminder that a 'lily-white' skin is no indicator of learning or accomplishment (and certainly not in Ireland, where a new international survey shows a quarter of all Irish adults are functionally illiterate); that asylum-seekers and even economic migrants ('now made to sound like dirty words'), might have something to contribute, even to smug Ireland; that the next time someone like herself fetches up at Dublin airport, immigration officials there might see more than 'a little brown woman' standing before them and dispense with the ritual humiliations. [...]

In her world travels to give lectures and promote her gardening and plant books, Mary is recognised and welcomed at many airports. But not Dublin: 'Every time I come back to the airport, it's always the same. No whites in front of me will be stopped. But I will be stopped, and the question, always, will be: "Where are you coming from?" That's before they look at the passport.' (The question is relevant to asylum-seekers who, under European law, must be processed in the country of first resort).

Aoife – again with the wry laugh – recalls how after a European trip last year, she and Matthew arrived back at Dublin.

'I go into the EU channel and Matthew, being American, into the non-EU channel. I should have been through well before him. But the guy stopped me, looked at me, and asked how long I had had citizenship. He hadn't even glanced at my passport, which has my place of birth – Dublin – written down. Eventually, he muttered something that didn't sound polite and let me go. The irony is that Matthew, a non-EU citizen, had been waved straight through.' [...]

Mary nods in agreement. 'Of course, people must ask questions. But where are the Irish smiles? What has happened to Irish courtesy? Why must they be so stonefaced?'

To Mary, official stone-faces are not new. Roll back 10 years to when she approached a Department of Justice official to seek a study visa for her 17-year-old nephew. 'I will never forget that girl who treated me with such contempt ...' she says, her voice trailing off. 'I then made an appointment to see somebody in charge. I lost my dignity, my pride, my arrogance as a high-caste Tamil ... I pleaded for a two-year visa. I said I would be paying his fees, that he would be going to a private school, that it wasn't in my culture to ask for hand-outs – and to this day, we never have sought handouts, in spite of three redundancies of my husband.

'I got the visa, through tears, beggings, pleadings. I had to do that and yet I am a citizen. I could not bring my mother here, who was found in a refugee camp. There was no procedure to bring a blood relative into this country. Why, as a citizen, can I not do this?' [...]

'Ireland has lived in this cocoon,' says Mary, 'and had this begging bowl mentality. And now we've emerged with an upside down begging bowl. Are we educating a whole person through our education system? If so, how can any normal, educated human being take pleasure in humiliating another?

'I had hoped that my child and grandchildren-to-come would have a sense of belonging in Ireland, but that has been removed from my confidence. Therefore I don't want them to come here. Why would I? To see them stopped at the airport and asked "Who are you?"

'My ashes shall be thrown into the sea, for the simple reason that I do not belong anymore. Ireland built me as a person and I am very, very thankful, but now they are robbing me of that. I do not regret a moment of my life here but the question is: do I belong here anymore?'

1. Give three examples of the racist treatment which Mary Toomey and her daughter Aoife have experienced in Ireland.
2. Aoife Toomey expresses her annoyance because she is expected 'to be thankful and humble and less visible' (l. 35). What do you think she is referring to and why does this bother her?
3. What does Mary Toomey mean when she says '... now we've emerged with an upside down begging bowl' (ll. 141–143)?
4. Can you understand Aoife's decision to leave Ireland – her home country – permanently and to go live in the USA? Would you have done the same? Explain your answer and discuss.
5. Imagine you are Aoife Toomey and write a letter to the editor of the *Irish Times* describing some of your experiences and expressing your concerns about racism.

6 *wry* (adj): showing that you are both amused and disappointed or annoyed **15** *populace* [ˈpɒpjələs ☆ ˈpɑːp-] (fml): all the people of a particular country or area **15** *reel at sth.:* feel very schocked or upset about sth. **16** *near-fatal* [-ˈfeɪtəl]: nearly leading to death **18** *Aoife* [iːfe] **21** *stab sb.:* attack sb. with a knife **24** *Trinity* = *Trinity College:* oldest and most prestigious university in Ireland, located in Dublin, founded in 1592 **37** *whinge* [wɪndʒ] (IrE infml) (derog): complain in an annoying way **39** *contempt:* Verachtung, Geringschätzung **40** *erosion:* gradual destruction or weakening of sth. over a period of time **41** *betrayal:* act of hurting sb. who trusts you, esp. by not being faithful or loyal **45** *caste:* (in Hindu society) system of dividing society into classes based on differences in family origin, rank or wealth **52–53** *do a PhD:* promovieren **58** Louth: county on the north-east border of the Irish Republic (cf. map, inside cover) **58** Kerry: county in the south-west of the Irish Republic **59** *Co Wexford* (abbr) = *County Wexford:* county on the eastern coast of the Irish Republic **59–60** *St Patrick's Day:* 17 March, an official holiday (in the Irish Republic) celebrating St Patrick (?385–461), the national saint of Ireland **60** *inundate sb. with sth.* [ˈ- - -]: give or send sb. so many things that they cannot deal with them all **65** *headhunt sb.:* find sb. who is suitable for a senior job and persuade them to leave their present job **71** *heritage* [ˈherɪtɪdʒ]: Erbe, Erbschaft **72** *carving* (n): Schnitzerei **74** *literate* [ˈlɪtərət] (adj): able to read and write **75** *prized* (adj): highly valued **79** *boast* (n): sth. that a person talks about in a very proud way, often to seem more important or clever **88** *fetch up* (IrE infml): arrive at a place without planning to **102** *first resort:* (here) place where asylum seekers arrived first **116** *nod:* nicken

The Holy Family

1 An Artist's View Micheal Farrell

In 1977 the Irish painter Micheal Farrell attracted attention in Ireland with the work shown below. In it Farrell makes use of certain icons of art history, such as Leonardo da Vinci's 'Universal Man', which revealed the Renaissance painter's view of the New Man, and Francois Boucher's 'Blonde Odalisque (Miss O'Murphy)' (1752), which shows a nude 14-year-old Irish girl believed to have been King Louis XV's lover. Farrell has also smuggled in a frog and his own face.

1. Make notes on your first reaction to the painting and the particular elements which affect you the most. Discuss your notes in class.
2. What do you associate with the term 'Madonna'? Speculate on why Farrell gave his painting the title 'Madonna Irlanda' and the subtitle 'The Very First Real Irish Political Picture'.
3. Farrell's painting caused a great deal of controversy in Ireland when it was first shown in 1977. What may have been some reasons for this reaction?

2 Irish Voices on Catholic Ireland Mary Kenny

In her book *Goodbye to Catholic Ireland* (2000) Mary Kenny recorded personal memories and impressions of the Catholic Church from prominent Irish citizens. The following are the words of three of them. Maeve Binchy, 63, is a best-selling author of popular fiction. John Banville, 58, also an accomplished novelist, was a pupil at the Christian Brothers, a Catholic boys school. And Andrea Corr, 29, a member of the pop group The Corrs, represents the younger generation of Irish Catholics.

Maeve Binchy

Like every other Irish child born around 1940, I thought that the Pope had been a guest at my parents' wedding. The papal blessing was there on the wall saying that William and Maureen had prostrated themselves at his feet, and I knew they had never been in Rome. I wasn't sure how he had been let out for the day, but guessed he must have worked something.

I thought the angelus rang at 12 noon and 6 p.m. in every country – how else would people know it was lunch time or tea time?

I was always ambitious and when I was young I wanted to be a saint. There would be a Saint Maeve's Day and children would have a holiday from school and have processions with statues of me all around the country. God was Irish and Our Lady was Irish and St Patrick was the Managing Director up there keeping our places ready for us.

And because I felt so strong, I also felt guilty about being bored by interminable sermons in a church full of coughing parishioners. Instead, I would talk to God in my head and tell Him about the world down here. Interpreting things for Him, and making endless requests. Like could He take my baby sister back. I knew I had prayed for one, but she was taking up too much time and too much attention away from me and I would have preferred a rabbit. Like that I assumed that the only reason I was fat was because God loved me so much, because I remembered that bit about whom the Lord loveth he persecutith. And being fat at school was a fair amount of persecution all right.

We had parents who loved us, a happy home, wonderful hard-working nuns who taught us well at the Holy Child Convent school, pleasant priests in the parish, so obviously our Irish childhood passed very well indeed. I used to read school stories and wonder where the nons *were* in them, thinking that all children *had* to be taught by nuns, otherwise it didn't take.

I never met a nun who slapped my fingers with a ruler, or was cruel. I never met a priest who threatened hell fire or excommunication. If there were Church scandals back then, and of course there must have been, we never heard of them.

We did have a distant relative, a priest who was rumoured to drink a little too much whiskey, but the main thrust of that was to ensure that he kept well away from driving a car. [...]

But as the years went on, everything changed. The teachings of the Second Vatican Council crept slowly in, the economy improved, the people could travel and come back rather than travel away for ever as emigrants. The wind of change that was the Sixties finally blew into Ireland, television opened up worlds far beyond our own. No longer was this comfortable safe little world, where everyone was Irish and Catholic and good, anything we could believe in.

Possibly because I was dealt a good hand with a very secure happy family life, I had no angst, resentment or rage when losing my own place in the Irish Heavenly Scene. I would *love* to believe it all again, the same way I would like a Tooth Fairy and Santa Claus. And maybe some day I will. But at the moment, if I were to try it would be like inventing a religion for myself, fooling myself and others into thinking I had a belief that is not there. I have nothing but envy for those who are still linked in. They think they will see their parents again, they think we might all be happy ever after, while I think it's a big sleep. Who would not envy the sureness and certainty of that wonderful Irish Catholic youth? [...]

John Banville

I grew up in the Fifties. I am appalled when people look back at the Fifties nostalgically. Wexord was a safe town. Our horizons were very near.

I wasn't beaten very much at the Christian Brothers. There were a few who were absolute savages – I remember one saying, after Wexford had won a hurling match, that we needn't feel any pride. It was a Wexford man who brought in the British. That was Dermot McMorrough (who was responsible for bringing in the Norman English). Yet I also remember wonderful Christian Brothers, when I was small.

At the end of every day there was one who used to read us *The Wind in the Willows*. There was another who used to bring his gramophone in and play us music – a wonderful man. I remember a large good-looking man who taught us, too. He was reading a poem – a love poem – and he went blank for a moment and said, 'You boys don't know what love is, but you will ...'. There was so much loss in that look, so much loss in his life. There were fine men amongst them.

The diocesan priest beat us far more. They were very confident of their power. I was lucky because I was clever and did my exams, so I didn't get beaten much. Once, I remember it happening. It would be three whacks on either hand as hard as he could. That was a Father Sheridan. He was a brute. There was another priest, a Father Larkin, who was absolutely wonderful. He was the English teacher who pushed me to write. I met him once, afterwards, at the airport: he was coming back from Peru where he would spend time on missions, with poor people.

There was a dark sexuality behind the beatings. There was an awful lot of homosexuality, between the boys and between the boys and the priests. I suppose there was a deep fear of women in the Irish Church. The most wounded, the most injured of the boys would become priests themselves, I think.

Yet I'm grateful for my background in Catholic Ireland. It brings a splendid baggage of grief for any writer. And I hate to see the way the country has become so materialistic now. We had a conference at *The Irish Times* where we were discussing who we would put on Nelson's Pillar if it were to be re-erected. I suggested Bishop Casey. He caused the whole collapse. The calmness with which the country took it, really, was amazing. The whole system just collapsed, and so quickly. I heard a Dublin woman saying to a child recently: 'If you don't fuckin' behave yourself, I'll send you to them paedophiles'.

Andrea Corr

The legacy of Catholic Ireland certainly does mean a lot to me. It is engraved in our society, although as a woman there are a lot of arguments I might have with the Church. The essentials are right. The Ten Commandments are right. But it's a man-made institution and mistakes are made. In the past, it sometimes left people with the sense of sin about sex and this affected young people in their married lives. Yet the moral standards in Ireland are good. We are lucky and I feel a sense of pride in the Ireland of my background. Irish values kept the family together, and of all the countries I have been to, I think of Ireland as one of the happiest.

Our father is very much a practising Catholic. Our mother – she was a very natural, earthy woman [Jean Corr sadly died in November 1999], and I think she would have had her criticisms of the Church. She wouldn't have thought that men in collars should tell her how to live her life. ... Yet the fundamentals of the Catholic Church remain right, and I cherish the lagacy. I had a very nice time at school [with the St Louis nuns]. A lot of our faith, though, is down to our parents.

For the future, the church will have to loosen up. The hypocrisy will have to go. It should definitely embrace all people. The Church should not be judgemental – we will all have to meet our own judgement. The Church should be comforting. It should be a helping thing. Life isn't easy for a lot of people, and the Church should be an anchor. We've all got the same sins, and the same sins as the people before us had, too. We should be honest about that.

A mass of people praying in a room together is just so bonding. It is so good for people to be able to do that. My father told us stories about sectarianism in the past, about how you couldn't go to a Protestant funeral. But I didn't experienced anything like that in my generation. I would bless myself passing a Protestant church just as much as I would bless myself passing a Catholic church. I consider every church holy.

2 *blessing* (n): Segen **3** *prostrate oneself* ['prɒstreɪt ☆ 'prɑːs-]: lie on the ground facing downwards **5** *work something* (IrE infml): arrange sth. **11** *St Patrick* (?385–461) national saint of Ireland **14** *interminable* [- '- - - -]: endless **14** *sermon:* predigt **14** *parishioner:* Gemeindemitglieder **20–21** *whom the Lord loveth he persecutith* (old-fashioned): (reference to the Bible, originally 'Whom the Lord loveth he chasteneth', Hebrews 12:6) the Lord punishes those who he loves **27** *it didn't take* (IrE infml): it didn't work **28** *ruler:* Lineal **33** *thrust of sth.:* main point of sth., esp. an argument, statement, etc. **35–36** *Second Vatican Council* (1962–1965): large-scale internal review of the Church's institutions which resulted in reformative measures to make the teachings more accessible to the modern world **36** *creep in:* gradually have an effect **42** *deal sb. a good hand:* (of card-playing) give sb. good playing cards; (here) give sb. an advantage **45** *Tooth Fairy:* fairy (= Fee) that leaves money for children while they sleep in exchange for a tooth that has come out **53** *Wexford:* town on the south-eastern coast of the Irish Republic **55** *savage* ['sævɪdʒ]: cruel and violent person **56** *hurling* (n): traditional Irish ball game, related to hockey but with different rules **57** *Dermot McMorrough:* King of Leinster, who was driven from Ireland in the 12th century; he appealed to Henry II for assistance in regaining his kingdom, which led to the Norman invasion of Ireland in 1170 AD **61** *The Wind in the Willows:* classic children's book by Kenneth Grahame, published in 1908 **64–6** *go blank:* show no feeling, understanding or interest **73** *brute:* man who treats people in an unkind, cruel way **83** *splendid* (old fashioned): excellent, very good **84** *grief:* sadness **86** *Nelson's Pillar:* former monument in the centre of Dublin to British military power, with a statue of the 19th-century British admiral Horatio Nelson; it was destroyed by Republicans in the Easter Rising of 1916 **87** *Bishop Casey = Bishop Eamon Casey* (born 1927): former Bishop of Galway, who was involved in a highly publicized scandal in 1992 **92** *legacy* ['legəsi]: situation that exists now because of past events, actions, etc. **93** *engrave sth.:* be sth. unforgettable because it has had such a strong effect **96** *Ten Commandments:* zehn Gebote **107** earthy: (of a person) open and direct **115** *be down to sb./sth.:* be caused by a person or thing **117** *hypocrisy* [hɪ'pɒkrəsi ☆ -'pɑːk-]: Heuchelei; Scheinheiligkeit **118** *embrace sb./sth.:* include sb./sth. **122** *anchor* ['æŋkə]: Anker **125** *bonding* (adj): causing people or groups to form a special connection with each other **126** *sectarianism:* strong support for one religious or political group, esp. when this leads to violence between groups **129** *bless oneself:* sich bekreuzigen

1. Summarize each speaker's attitude towards the church.
2. Describe the perspective which Binchy takes and explain how she makes this perspective amusing for the reader. Use examples from the text.
3. What does John Banville mean when he says that his Irish Catholic background 'brings a splendid baggage of grief for any writer' (ll. 83–84)?
4. To what extent is Andrea Corr's view of Catholicism in Ireland unusual for a young pop star? Do you think many pop stars in your country might say something like this? Discuss in class.

Changing Values in Ireland

Sunday mass at a Catholic church in Belfast.

The role of the Church

Ireland is an overwhelmingly Catholic country. Over 90% of the Republic of Ireland's population belongs to the Catholic Church (in Northern Ireland only 40%, though this minority makes up the largest religious group). Although weekly church attendance is very high in a European context (around 60%), it has fallen significantly since the early 1990s and there has been a downturn in the numbers of those joining the clergy. A survey in 1998 found a loss in confidence in religious leaders since the beginning of the 1990s. This is partly the result of a series of individual scandals involving priests who were convicted of sexually abusing children. Another cause are cases involving priests who were allowed to stay on in their positions despite complaints of sexual abuse. Particularly difficult for critics and the general public is the long time it has taken the Catholic hierarchy to respond to these cases and the perceived lack of sympathy and help for the victims.

Many young Catholics no longer place importance on regular church-going. While many still attend church for weddings, baptisms, funerals and Christmas mass, it is otherwise no longer part of their daily life. However, according to the survey mentioned above, belief in God, life after death and heaven is still very high. Although there has been a great loss of trust in the institution, the spiritual side of religion remains very much alive.

Despite these changes, the Church continues to play an important societal role in Ireland. In education, for example, Catholic schools at both the primary and secondary levels have a long tradition. And in health care, religious orders run well-established hospices.

Views on love and relationships

Certain issues show clearly that Ireland is not the stereotypically priest-dominated society of god-fearing religiosity it once was. Bans on contraception, homosexuality and divorce have been removed and sexual morality is increasingly seen as a private matter. In the case of divorce, it was prohibited under the Constitution of 1937. But attitudes started to change in the 1970s. In a referendum held on 24th November, 1995, the Irish voted by a slim margin of 50.3% to 49.7% to lift the ban on divorce. The clearest majority was in Dublin and other urban centres. It was a victory of the urban over the agricultural and more conservative Ireland and, of course, over the Church. The new divorce legislation has not, however, led to a large number of divorces. A couple may only divorce if they have been separated for four years and if there is 'no reasonable prospect of a reconciliation'. Interestingly, more women apply for legal separations than men – in 1999, women outnumbered men by 4 to 1 (from a total of almost 2500). There appears to be a similar trend with divorce applications.

Whose life is it?

Abortion was made a criminal offence under Irish law in 1861. Today Ireland continues to have some of the most restrictive abortion regulations in the world. Change has been taking place, however, especially in the past decade, as the result of deeply divisive cases of teenage rape victims who, under the law, were forced to continue their pregnancies. Decisions by the Irish Supreme Court and by constitutional referenda now ensure that a pregnancy can be legally terminated if 'such termination is necessary to save the life of the mother'. Abortion facilities are, however, not provided in Ireland. This has resulted in an extremely high number of Irish women having abortions in England (in 1999 more than 6000 women – and this is only the official number).

Left and directly above: Campaigning in the run-up to the abortion referendum of March 2002.

3 Close to Home Colm Toíbín

Colm Toíbín's novel *The Heather Blazing* (1992) tells the story of Eamon Redmond, a much admired and successful High Court judge in Dublin. He is happily married to Carmel and has two children, Niamh and Donel, who are both grown-up. The family spends most summers in a beautiful house in Cush on the western Irish coast. As summer approaches once again, a single event marks a critical shift in Eamon's life and in his personal relationships.

He woke during the night and went downstairs to his study. He had been dreaming, but now the dream had escaped him. He went into the kitchen and took some cold water from a plastic bottle in the fridge. He sat at the kitchen table for a while and then went back into the study. It was a warm night.

He sat at his desk and looked down at the judgement he had written in longhand on foolscap pages. It was ready to be delivered. He wondered for a moment if he should have it typed, but he was worried about it being leaked. No one knew about it; even as he sat down to write it himself he did not know what he would say, what he would decide. There was so little to go on, no real precedent, no one obviously guilty. Neither of the protagonists in the case had broken the law. And that was all he knew: the law, its letter, its traditions, its ambiguities, its codes. Here, however, he was being asked to decide on something more fundamental and now he realized that he had failed and he felt afraid.

He took a biro from a drawer and began to make squiggles on a pad of paper. What was there beyond the law? 'Law'; he wrote the word. There was natural justice. He wrote the two words down and put a question mark after them. And beyond that again there was the notion of right and wrong, the two principles which governed everything and came from God. 'Right' and 'wrong'; he wrote the two words down and then put brackets around them and the word 'God' in capitals beside them.

Somehow here in the middle of the night with the moths and midges drawn to the window, the idea of God seemed more clearly absurd to him than ever before; the idea of a being whose mind put order on the universe, who watched over things, and whose presence gave the world a morality which was not based on self-interest, seemed beyond belief. He wondered how people put their faith in such a thing, and yet he unterstood that the courts and the law ultimately depended for their power on such an idea. He crossed out the word 'God'. He felt powerless and strange as he went back to read random passages of his judgement. He decided to go to bed and sleep some more: maybe he would be more relaxed about his judgement in the morning.

Carmel did not stir in the bed when he came into the bedroom, but he knew that she had woken. When he got into bed he put his arms around her. She kissed him gently on the neck and then turned away from him, letting him

snuggle against her. She fell back asleep, and he lay there for a while holding her until he grew drowsy and fell asleep as well.

He was wakened by the alarm clock and reached across her to turn it off. They both lay without moving or speaking, as though still asleep.

'Are you in court today?' she finally asked, almost whispering.

'Yes,' he said.

'Do you have a full day?'

'There's a lot of work to get through.'

Another last day of term; another year gone by. He hoped that all the urgent applications for injunctions would go elsewhere. He knew that the press would be in his court today. This case was newsworthy. He hated the journalists' faces looking up at him, eager for something instant which they could grasp and simplify. He snoozed for a while and when he woke he found that Carmel had left her bed. He moved over to her side and lay in her heat until he knew that it was time to get up.

It was a fine morning. Thin wisps of white cloud hung in the sky like smoke, and the sun was already strong. He realized as he tested the water in the shower that he would like to get into his car now and drive with Carmel to Cush and never set foot in the court again.

She was still in her dressing-gown when he came downstairs. She poured tea for him.

'I think everything is ready now,' she said. 'Are you looking forward to getting away?'

'Yes, I am. I was just thinking that I'd be delighted never to set foot in the court again.'

'You'll feel different at the end of the summer.'

He went into his study again and sat at the desk. He thought that he should read the judgement over again before going into the court, but he could not face it. He felt unsure about it, but as he left the house and drove into the city the uncertainty became deep unease. It was not yet nine o'clock when he arrived at the Four Courts, and he was not due to deliver his judgement until eleven, or maybe later, depending on what injunctions were being sought.

The line of reasoning in his judgement was clear, he thought. It had not been written in a hurry; evening after evening he had sat in his study and drafted it, working out the possibilities, checking the evidence and going over the facts. Even so, he was still not sure.

He stood at the window of his chambers and looked out at the river which was low now because of the tide and because of the good summer. He watched a boy moving between lorries and cars on a horse, riding bareback with confidence. When the lights changed to green, the boy and his horse joined the flow of traffic towards Capel Street.

He had taken the judgement from his briefcase and placed it on the table. He went over and looked at it again. The case had happened in one of the border towns. A lot of people must live on the edge there, he thought, with strange upheavals, odd comings and goings. But this had nothing to do with the case, as far as he knew. The case was simple: a sixteen-year-old girl attending a convent school had become pregnant and been expelled. She was due to have the baby over the summer and wished to return to the school for her final year, but the school had made it clear that she would not be re-admitted. The girl and her mother sought a court order instructing the school to take her back.

The girl was clever, according to the school reports which had been produced in evidence. Her becoming pregnant had been a great trauma and she had confided in nobody until it became obvious. Both the girl and her mother had given evidence. The mother seemed surprisingly young, but had been very confident in the witness box as she told of her visits to the school to talk to the principal and her long discussions with her daughter about her pregnancy and her future. She seemed sincere and deeply upset about her daughter's expulsion.

It would have been easier for everyone, she said, if her daughter had had an abortion. But because they decided to have the child and bring it up in the town, her daughter was being made to suffer. She would have to go to the Vocational School or travel every day to another town. She was being victimized, stigmatized, her mother said. She told the court that the principal had been more interested in keeping the pregnancy a secret than in her daughter's welfare or the welfare of the unborn child.

The daughter was a smaller, softer version of her mother, but just as articulate and just as sure that an injustice had been done to her. She liked the school, she said, she had a good relationship with all of her teachers, she expected to go to university after her final year. She told the court about her worry when she thought she might be pregnant, how she hoped she would have a miscarriage and wondered if she could get away and have an abortion without anyone discovering. When her mother found out, she said, she told her that all the family would support her. Her father had been upset for a few days but he said nothing bad to her.

The principal was new, she said, she had replaced a nun who had run the school for years. She was young and everybody liked her. So she was not afraid when she was called into the office. But she was very surprised, the girl told the court, when she was informed that she could not come back to the school that term. It was a few days later that the principal told her mother that she would not be allowed back to the school the following year. She was shocked by this and hurt, the girl said. She didn't want to go out and began to feel ashamed and depressed.

She told counsel for the school that she knew what she had done was wrong. And she agreed that it was a bad example for younger girls, especially in a Catholic school. She had told everyone she was sorry, she said. No one wanted to expel the boy, she said, although some people knew who he was. She felt being expelled from the school stigmatized her.

He had spent three days listening to the case. The principal could only have been in her late twenties. She, too, was calm, assured and articulate. She was employed to run a Catholic school, she said. It was an educational establishment, but with a very specific ethos. She was prepared to forgive anybody a transgression, she said, and it was for God, not her, to judge, but she had to protect the school's ethos. There were, she told the court, great pressures on the girls in a changing world, but some things were still not acceptable to her as principal, to her board of management or to the majority of the parents. She had the right to decide if a girl should be expelled and she had decided to exercise that right.

Parents who had children in the school spoke for both sides. Some said that the girl should be forgiven and treated as a normal student in her final year. Others said that a teenage pregnancy should not be looked upon as normal or acceptable, and allowing the girl to return to school would have an abiding effect on her fellow students.

Eamon was aware as the case went on that the costs were rising and if the girl and her family lost it would be a great financial blow to them. He was disturbed by the case, which was widely reported on radio, television and in the newspapers. He remembered how calm the young girl had been, how vulnerable. He realized that this was one of the few cases he had heard where both sides were clearly telling the truth and were not afraid of the truth. All the witnesses were sincere, no one wished to hide anything.

He listened carefully to the counsel's submissions about various articles of the Constitution, but there was no argument about facts or truth, guilt or innocence. In the end he was not the legal arbiter, because there were so few legal issues at stake. Most of the issues raised in the case were moral: the right of an ethos to prevail over the right of an individual. Basically, he was being asked to decide how life should be conducted in a small town. He smiled to himself at the thought and shook his head.

As he worked on the judgement, he realized more than ever that he had no strong moral views, that he had ceased to believe in anything. But he was careful in writing the judgement not to make this clear. The judgement was the only one which he could have given: it was cogent, well argued and, above all, plausible.

He went to the window again and stood there looking out. How hard it was to be sure! It was not simply the case, and the questions it raised about society and morality, it was the world in which these things happened which left him uneasy, a world in which opposite values lived so close to each other. Which could claim a right to be protected?

He went over to his bookshelf and took down the sacred text: *Bunreacht na hEireann*, the Irish Constitution. This contained the governing principles to which the law was subject. The preamble was clear about the

Christian nature of the state, it specifically referred to the Holy Trinity. He thought about it again, how the school had a duty to defend Christian principles, and indeed a right to do so, under its own articles of association and also under the general guidance of the Constitution.

Surely these rights and duties were greater than any rights a single individual, whose presence in the school might undermine the school's ethos and principles, could lay claim to?

His tipstaff came with tea. He began to think again. He wrote down three words in a note-pad: charity, mercy, forgiveness. These words had no legal status, they belonged firmly to the language of religion, but they had a greater bearing on the case than any set of legal terms. Opposite them he wrote three other words: transgression, sin, scandal. He sighed.

One other matter began to preoccupy him. The family, according to the Constitution, was the basic unit in society. He read the words in the Constitution: 'a moral institution possessing inalienable rights, antecedent and superior to all positive law'. What was a family? The Constitution did not define a family, and at the time it was written in 1937 the term was perfectly understood: a man, his wife and their children. But the Constitution was written in the present tense, it was not his job to decide what certain terms – he wrote 'certain terms' in his note-pad, underlined it and wrote 'uncertain terms' below that – such as 'the family' had meant in the past. It was his job to define and redefine these terms now. Could not a girl and her child be a family? And if they were, did the girl have rights arising from her becoming a mother, thus creating a family, greater than the rights of any institution?

He thought about it for a while and the consternation it would cause among his colleagues, a broadening of the concept of the family. The girl would have to win then, and the school lose. The idea seemed suddenly plausible, but it would need a great deal of thought and research. It had not been raised as a possibility by counsel for the girl and her mother. Lawyers, he thought, knew that he was not the sort of judge who would entertain such far-fetched notions in his court.

If he were another person he could write the judgement, but as eleven o'clock grew near he knew that the verdict he had written out on his foolscap pages was the one he would deliver, and it would be viewed by his colleagues as eminently sensible and well reasoned. But he was still unhappy about the case because he had been asked to interpret more than the law, and he was not equipped to be a moral arbiter. He was not certain about right and wrong, and he realized that this was something he would have to keep hidden from the court.

7 *foolscap* (BE): large size of writing paper **8** *leak sth.:* make sth. (esp. information) known to the public that should remain secret **11** *precedent* ['presɪdənt]: action or decision which is seen as an example or a model for similar situations in the future **16** *squiggle:* Schnörkel **19** *notion:* idea **23** *midge:* Stechmücke **28** *faith:* trust **31** *random* (adj): chosen without any particular plan or reason **46** *injunction:* official order given by a court of law to do or not do sth. **49** *snooze:* sleep for a short while **52** *wisp:* long thin line of smoke or cloud **55** *Cush:* (in the novel) coastal village where the Redmond family spend their summer holidays **80** *border town:* town on or near the border between two countries (here, the Irish Republic and Northern Ireland) **81** *upheaval:* big change which causes problems **83** *convent school* ['- -]: school which is run by nuns **83** *expel sb.:* officially make sb. leave a school or organization **90** *confide in sb.:* tell sb. sth. strictly private **99** *Vocational School:* Berufsschule **100** *victimize sb.:* make sb. suffer unfairly **100** *stigmatize sb.:* treat sb. in a way that makes them feel bad or unimportant **108** *miscarriage:* Fehlgeburt **120** *counsel:* lawyer or group of lawyers representing sb. in a court of law **129** *transgression* (fml): act of going beyond the limit of what is morally or legally acceptable **138** *abiding* (adj): lasting **144** *vulnerable:* easily hurt **147** *submission:* statement that is made to a judge in a court of law **49** *arbiter* (fml): person with the authority to make judgements and decide what will be done or accepted **157** *cogent* ['kəʊdʒənt ☆ 'koʊ-] (fml): stichhaltig, überzeugend **166** *subject to sth.* (adj): under the authority of sb./sth. **166** *preamble* [pri'æmbl]: introduction to a book or written document **174** *tipstaff:* court official responsible for keeping things in the court in order **175** *mercy:* Gnade **181** *inalienable* (fml): that cannot be taken away from you **181** *antecedent* (fml) [ˌæntɪ'si:dnt]: previous **182** *positive law:* written corpus of laws and orders which do not have the legal status of constitutional principles or natural rights **191** *consternation* (fml): surprise, shock

1. What are the facts of the case which Eamon Redmond has to pass judgement on?

2. Describe the Judge's thoughts and feelings leading up to his final judgement. Why is the decision he has to make such a difficult one?

3. Later in the novel it is revealed that Eamon's unmarried daughter Niamh was pregnant, too, and now has a baby. What does this fact suggest about Eamon and his relationship to Niamh?

4. On the basis of the information in the text, speculate on Eamon's final decision. Give reasons for your view.

5. Group work: Put together a written statement in which you either defend or condemn the school's decision to expel the girl. Then prepare to argue your group's position in a classroom debate. Begin by reading your statement to the opposing group.

4 D'yeh Want to Keep It? Roddy Doyle

In his first three novels, known as the Barrytown trilogy, Irish author Roddy Doyle follows the Rabbittes, a North Dublin working-class family of eight, through a series of depressing if somewhat comical conflicts. *The Snapper* (1990) is his second novel in this literary cycle. In the novel Doyle tries to reflect the idiom of his fictional heroes. Written almost entirely in dialogue, his prose is full of the slang, colloquialisms and vulgarisms of the Irish working class. In this opening scene, Sharon Rabbitte brings home shocking news.

Sharon (left), Jimmy Sr. and Veronica (middle) in the film version of *The Snapper* (1993).

– You're wha'? said Jimmy Rabbitte Sr.

He said it loudly.

– You heard me, said Sharon

Jimmy Jr was upstairs in the boys' room doing his D.J. practice. Darren was in the front room watching Police Academy II on the video. Les was out. Tracy and Linda, the twins, were in the front room annoying Darran. Veronica, Mrs Rabbitte, was sitting opposite Jimmy Sr at the kitchen table.

Sharon was pregnant and she'd just told her father that she thought she was. She'd told her mother earlier, before the dinner.

– Oh – my Jaysis, said Jimmy Sr.

He looked at Veronica. She looked tired. He looked at Sharon again.

– That's shockin', he said.

Sharon said nothing.

– Are yeh sure? said Jimmy Sr.

– Yeah. Sort of.

– Wha'?
– Yeah.
Jimmy Sr wasn't angry. He probably wouldn't be either, but it all seemed very unfair.
– You're only nineteen, he said.
– I'm twenty.
– You're only twenty.
– I know what age I am, Daddy.
– Now, there's no need to be gettin' snotty, said Jimmy Sr.
– Sorry, said Sharon.
She nearly meant it.
– I'm the one tha' should be gettin' snotty, said Jimmy Sr.
Sharon made herself smile. She was happy with the way things were going so far.
– It's shockin', said Jimmy Sr again, – so it is. Wha' do you think o' this?
He was talking to Veronica.
– I don't know, said Veronica.
– Is tha' the best yeh can do, Veronica?
– Well, what do YOU think?
Jimmy Sr creased his face and held it that way for a second.
– I don't know, he said. – I should give ou', I suppose. An' throw a wobbler or somethin'. But – what's the point?
Veronica nodded. She looked very tired now.
Jimmy Sr continued.
– If she was –
He turned to Sharon.
– You should've come to us earlier – before, yeh know – an' said you were goin' to get pregnant.
The three of them tried to laugh.
– Then we could've done somethin' abou' it. — My God, though.
No one said anything. Then Jimmy Sr spoke to Sharon again.
– You're absolutely sure now? Positive?
– Yeah, I am. I done –
– Did, said Veronica.
– I did the test.
– The test? said Jimmy Sr. – Oh. – Did yeh go in by yourself.
– Yeah, said Sharon.
– Did yeh? Fair play to yeh, said Jimmy Sr. – I'd never've thought o' tha'.
Sharon and Veronica looked at each other, and grinned quickly.
Jimmy Sr got down to business.
– Who was it?
– Wha'? — Oh. I don't know.
– Ah now, Jaysis –!
– No, I do know.
– Well, then?
– I'm not tellin'.
Jimmy Sr could feel himself getting a bit angry now. That was better.

– Now, look –

They heard Jimmy Jr from up in the boys' room.

– THIS IS JIMMY RABBITTE – ALL – OVER – IRELAND.

– Will yeh listen to tha' fuckin' eejit, said his father.

– Leave him alone, said Veronica.

Jimmy Sr stared at the ceiling.

– I don't know.

Then he turned to Sharon again.

– Why won't yeh tell us?

Sharon said nothing. Jimmy Sr saw her eyes filling with water.

– Don't start tha', he told her. – Just tell us.

– I can't, Sharon told the table.

– Why not?

– I just can't, righ'.

Jimmy Sr looked across at Veronica and shook his head. He'd never been able to cope with answers like that. If Sharon had been one of the boys he'd have walloped her.

Veronica looked worried now. She wasn't sure she really wanted to know the answer.

– Is he married? Jimmy Sr asked.

– Oh my God, said Veronica.

– No, he's not! said Sharon.

– Well, that's somethin', I suppose, said Jimmy Sr.

– Then why –

Veronica started crying.

– Ah Veronica, stop tha'.

[...]

He looked at Veronica. She just looked tired again.

– This is an awful shock, Sharon, he said. – Isn't it, Veronica?

– Definitely.

– Make us a cup o' tea there, love, will yeh.

– Make it yourself, said Veronica.

– I'll make it, said Sharon.

– Good girl, said Jimmy Sr. – Mind yourself against the table there. Good girl.

– You're sure now he's not married?

– Yeah, he's not, said Sharon, at the sink.

– Then why won't yeh tell us then?

– Look, said Sharon.

She turned to face him.

– I can't, an' I'm not goin' to.

She turned back to plug in the kettle.

– Will he marry you? Jimmy Sr asked her.

– No. I don't think so.

– The louser. That's cheatin', tha' is.

– It's not a game! said Veronica.

– I know, I know tha', Veronica. But it's his fault as much as Sharon's. Whoever he is. – It was his flute tha' –

– Daddy!
– Well, it was.
– It's no wonder they all talk the way they do, Veronica gave out to Jimmy Sr.
– Ah, lay off, Veronica, will yeh.
They heard a scream from the front room.
– Hang on till I sort this young fella ou', said Jimmy Sr.
He marched out of the kitchen.
– He's taking it well, said Veronica.
– Yeah, said Sharon. – So are you.
– Ah sure –
– I was afraid you'd throw me ou'.
– I never thought of that, mind you. – It's not right though, said Veronica.
She looked straight at Sharon.
– I suppose it's not, said Sharon.
immy Sr came back, rubbing his hands and calling Darren a sneaky little bastard. He sat down and saw the tea waiting for him.
– Aah, lovely.
He sipped.
– Fuck! – Sorry, Veronica; excuse me. It's very hot.
– He's started saying Excuse me. After twenty-two years.
– Good luck, Jimmy Jr roared from the front door, and then he slammed it.
– He shuts the door like a normal man annyway. That's somethin', I suppose.
– He's alrigh', said Sharon.
Jimmy Sr now said something he'd heard a good few times on the telly.
– D'yeh want to keep it?
– Wha' d'yeh mean?
– D'yeh – d'you want to keep it, like?
– He wants to know if you want to have an abortion, said Veronica. – The eejit.
– I do not! said Jimmy Sr.
This was true. He was sorry now he'd said it.
– There's no way I'd have an abortion, said Sharon.
– Good. You're right.
– Abortion's murder.
– It is o' course.
Then he thought of something and he had to squirt his tea back into the cup. He could hear his heart. And feel it.
He looked at Sharon.
– He isn't a black, is he?
– No!
He believed her. The three of them started laughing.
– One o' them students, yeh know, Jimmy Sr explained. – With a clatter o' wives back in Africa.
– Stop that.
Jimmy Sr's tea was finished.
– That was grand, Sharon, thanks, he said. – An' you're def'ny not goin' to tell us who it is?
– No. – Sorry.

– Never mind the Sorry. – I think you should tell us. I'm not going to kill him or annythin'.
Sharon said nothing.
Jimmy Sr pushed his chair back from the table.
– There's no point in anny more talkin' then, I suppose.
Your mind's obviously made up, Sharon.
He stood up.
– A man needs a pint after all tha', he said.

d'yeh: do you **1** *wha':* what **10** *Jaysis:* Jesus; used to express intense surprise, esp. at sth. unpleasant **14** *yeh:* you **24** *snotty* (infml): rude **27** *tha':* that **30** *o':* of **35** *crease sth.:* make an expression with your face that causes lines in the skin **36** *ou':* out **36** *give out* (sl): become upset **36** *an':* and **36** *throw a wobbler* (sl): einen Wutanfall haben **42** *goin':* going **45** *somethin':* something **45** *abou':* about **53** *fair play to you* (IrE sl): well done **55** *get down to business:* become serious **66** *fucking* (infml) (vulg): verdammt **66** *eejit* (IrE sl): idiot **76** *righ':* right **79** *wallop sb.* (infml): hit sb. **106** *louser* (IrE sl): mean person **109** *flute* (sl vulg): penis **113** *lay off* (infml): used to tell sb. to stop doing sth. **115** *hang on* (infml): wait a moment **115** *sort sb. out* (infml): deal with sb. who is causing problems, esp. by punishing or attacking them **115** *fella* (sl): fellow **124** *sneaky* (infml): behaving in a secret and sometimes dishonest way **127** *sip sth.:* etwas in kleinen Schlucken trinken **133** *telly* (IrE, BE infml): television **144** *squirt sth.:* (hier) etwas spucken **150** *clatter* (sl): large number of sth. **154** *def'ny:* definitely **164** *pint* (IrE): pint of beer (esp. in a pub)

1. What sort of family are the Rabbittes?
2. Describe the attitudes of Jimmy Sr., Veronica and Sharon towards Sharon's pregnancy. What does this tell you about each of the characters?
3. What is the function of the narrative passages in Doyle's text? Give examples to illustrate your answer.
4. Comment on Sharon's statement: 'Abortion's murder' (l. 142)

Troubles and Hopes

1 Mother Ireland, Mother Ulster Rita Duffy

Ireland is traditionally personified as a protective mother and the Irish people as her children. Northern Irish artist Rita Duffy takes up this theme in two paintings which comment on the island's two dominant cultures.

'Mother Ireland', 1989

1. Write down your personal reaction to the paintings in a few sentences.
2. **a** Describe and analyse the two mother representations. Consider individual characteristics such as facial expression, colour, physical build, position, clothing, etc.
b Speculate about what these characteristics might symbolize.
3. Look at the pictorial elements in the foreground and/or background of each painting. What specific features of life in the Irish Republic and in Northern Ireland might they represent?

'Mother Ulster', 1989

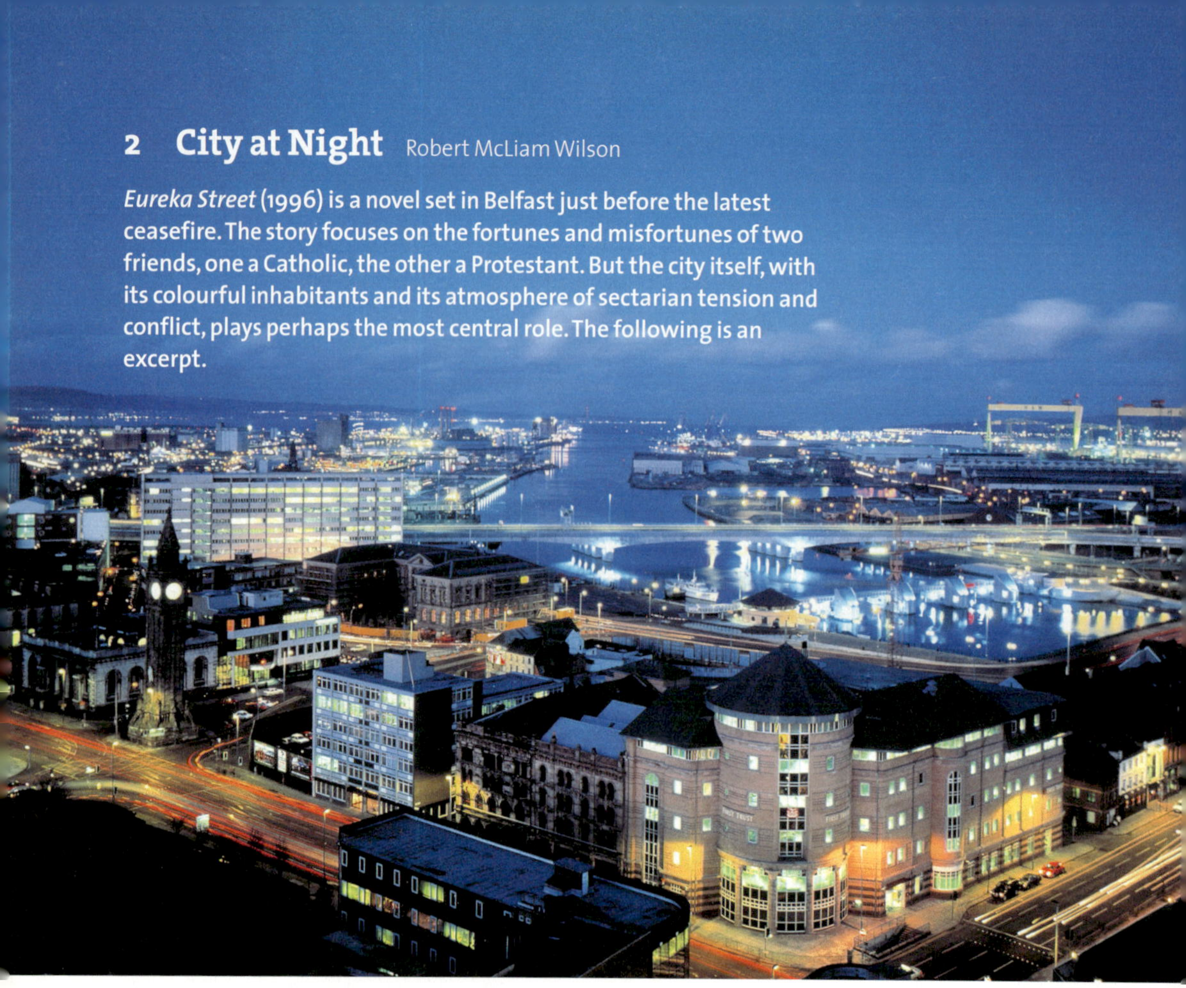

2 City at Night

Robert McLiam Wilson

Eureka Street (1996) is a novel set in Belfast just before the latest ceasefire. The story focuses on the fortunes and misfortunes of two friends, one a Catholic, the other a Protestant. But the city itself, with its colourful inhabitants and its atmosphere of sectarian tension and conflict, plays perhaps the most central role. The following is an excerpt.

The city rises and falls like music, like breathing. The sleeping streets feel free. The southside shopfronts and the streetlit sidewalks echo empty. Near Hope Street, a stray drinker walks late and wavy. In a small house in Mayard, a thin man lies sleepless and old. On Carmel Street, a dark young woman stalks fearfully in slippers, looking for her cat. There are small events everywhere. On Cedar Avenue, on Arizona Street, Sixth Street and Electric Street, the Royal Ulster Constabulary stand around in damp little groups, keeping an eye on nothing, stopping infrequent cars, checking licences, radioing control. Hello, Control?

Under street-lamps by all the city's walls, writing gleams: IRA, INLA, UVF, UFF, OTG. The city keeps its walls like a diary. In this staccato shorthand, the walls tell of histories and hatreds, shrivelled and bleached with age. *Qui a terre a guerre*, the walls say.

Posters and billboards flap in a hundred little winds. They proclaim concerts, religious meetings, theatres, religious meetings, consumer goods and religious meetings. On Brunswick Street a ragged orange poster flaps. 'The Reverend Ramsden's Travelling Cathedral & Disco, Formal Dress, No Catholics', it says.

On some poles, flags perch. From some windows they hang, upon the tops of certain tower blocks they flutter, these flags. There are a thousand flags, but five mere colours and only two designs. Green, white, gold, red and blue. The two three-coloured emblems of difference.

Throughout the city, bunches of flowers lie. They are grouped on pavements, in doorways or they are wedged between railings. The city is dotted with these false little gardens. The flowers bright and new in their wrapping paper, or weary and wilting with age. Any long walk through the city takes you past one or more of these sites. The citizens have placed these flowers on the spots where other citizens have been murdered. If the flowers are old, you pass and wonder who died there. You always fail to remember.

It is only late at night, if you stand up high, that you can see the city as one thing, as a single phenomenon. While all sleep, the daytime jumble is unified and, geographically at any rate, the city seems a single thing. You can see it ringed by its circles of black basalt, mountains, cliffs and plateaux. You can see the dark sea in the wide bay lapping right up to the foot of the metropolis, wetting its very heart.

You can see that Belfast is, quite literally, a dump. Its core is built on level land that simply wasn't there two hundred years before. Earth was dumped into the sea and Belfast was built there. Slob land, reclamation. The city is a raised beach, an abutment. The townsfolk say it rose from the water like some god but the truth is that it was dumped in the sea but didn't sink.

Belfast is Rome with more hills; it is Atlantis raised from the sea. And from anywhere you stand, from anywhere you look, the streets glitter like jewels, like small strings of stars.

Some say it is a city of 279,000 people, 130,000 men and 149,000 women, and that these people are squashed into 11,489 hectares. Some say that there are half a million souls there – Greater Belfast is Belfast too. Two cathedrals, some docks, a harbour, many hills and mountains. A sea-level town on the lip of the land.

However many, whatever size, it is magical. This night, the streets smell stale and tired, the air is full of regret and desire. Time seems passing and passed. The city feels how it feels to grow old.

However magical or glittering, you can read the signs. You have seen the flags, the writing on the walls and the pavement flowers. This is a city where people are prepared to kill and die for a few pieces of coloured cloth. These are the standards of two peoples with a four- or eight-hundred-year-old difference, national and religious. It is an illogic, a conundrum that corrupts the blood here. There is no revolution, only deadly convolution.

But deep at night Belfast whispers in cool breaths that hatred is something like God. You can't see what you can't see, but if you fight and follow it blindly enough, it will keep you warm at nights.

As your eye roams the city (as your eyes must, as our eyes, those democratic unideological things, always will, giving witness, testimony), you see that there is indeed a division in the people here. Some call it religion, some call it politics. but the most reliable, the most ubiquitous division is money. Money is the division you can always put your money on.

You see leafy streets and you see leafless streets. You can imagine leafy lives and leafless ones. In the plump suburbs and the concrete districts your eyes see some truths, some real difference. The scars and marks of violence reside in only one type of place. Many of the populace seem to live well. Many prosper while many suffer.

Belfast is a city that has lost its heart. A shipbuilding, rope-making, linen-weaving town. It builds no ships, makes no rope and weaves no linen. Those trades died. A city can't survive without something to do with itself.

But at night, in so many ways, complex and simple, the city is proof of a God. This place often feels like the belly of the universe. It is a place much filmed but little seen. Each street, Hope, Chape, Chichester and Chief, is busy with the moving marks of the dead thousands who have stepped their lengths. They leave their vivid smell on the pavements, bricks, doorways and in the gardens. In this city, the natives live in a broken world – broken but beautiful.

Opposite: Until 1998 British soldiers were a familiar feature on Belfast's streets. Above: The aftermath of a bombing in Belfast in September 2000.

3 *stray:* separated from other people of the same kind **4** *stalk:* (here) walk quietly and self-consciously **6–7** *Royal Ulster Constabulary:* Northern Irish mainly Protestant police force **10** *INLA* (abbr) = *Irish National Liberation Army:* ultra-radical wing of the IRA (Irish Republican Army) **10** *UVF* (abbr) = *Ulster Volunteer Force:* radical militant Protestant group **11** *UFF* (abbr) = *Ulster Freedom Fighters:* radical militant Protestant group **11** *OTG:* (in the novel) fictitious abbreviation which stands for nothing, or for those Belfast people who do not care about the political conflict in their town **12** *shrivelled* (adj): (here) having become reduced in size and strength **12** *bleached* (adj): (here) less significant **12–13** *qui a terre a guerre* (French): those who have land have war **19** *perch on sth.:* stand on top of sth. **24** *wedge sth. between sth.:* put or squeeze sth. tightly into a narrow space between two things **26** *wilting* (adj): verwelkend **36** *dump* (n): place where waste material (here: earth) is unloaded **39** *slob* (infml): (here) not real, artificial **39** *reclamation* [ˌrekləˈmeɪʃn]: transforming of unused land or sea into productive and useful land **40** *abutment* (fml): area bordering on the sea **53** *stale:* no longer fresh, old **69** *conundrum:* confusing question or problem **71–72** *convolution* (fml): thing that is very complex and difficult to follow **80** *roam:* move without destination or aim **89** *ubiquitous* [juːˈbɪkwɪtəs]: seeming to be everywhere

1. Several street scenes in the text give an indication of the city's troubles (cf. ll. 16–28). List the scenes and describe them in your own words.
2. How does the narrator portray Belfast at night? Consider, for example, the mood and atmosphere.
3. According to the text, what divides the people of Belfast more than anything else? Explain.
4. Using examples from the text, describe the narrator's point of view. Explain how this point of view relates to his attitude towards the conflict.
5. Discuss the significance of the narrator's statement 'hatred is something like God' (ll. 68–69) in the context of Northern Ireland. To what extent do you think religion can be a source of hatred?

Bloody Sunday and the Official Inquiries

PARAS THIRTEEN, the walls said, BOGSIDE NIL
– from 'Casualty', Seamus Heaney

Like a bitter sports commentary, the graffiti quoted by the Irish poet documents the grim events of 30 January, 1972, a date which became a landmark in Irish history and a turning point in the Northern-Irish conflict. At a protest march which had begun peacefully, 13 men and boys were shot dead by British paratroopers, another man died later from his injuries, and 13 other people were wounded. Catholics in the city of Londonderry (known as Derry to Catholics) had organized a march to protest new laws that allowed police to intern suspects without trial. Public demonstrations had also been banned by legal order. The roughly 3000 marchers passed through the Bogside area of the city, which had been a nationalist 'no go area' for British troops for months beforehand. Paratroopers confronted demonstrators there and, after some began throwing rocks and bottles, the soldiers opened fire on the crowd.

The news of the shootings spread around the world, and the British Government immediately set up an official inquiry, which was led by England's Lord Chief Justice, Lord Widgery. While evidence showed that, in Widgery's words, 'none of the deceased or wounded is proved to have been shot whilst handling a firearm or bomb', Widgery accepted the statements of the paratroopers that they had only fired after being fired at first. Although civilian eyewitnesses reported that this was not the case, in his final report Widgery declared the soldiers innocent of any wrongdoing. Lord Widgery was heavily

Left and above: scenes from the Bogside area of Londonderry on Bloody Sunday.

criticized for not addressing a number of inconsistencies and for not considering all the evidence available at the inquiry. Nevertheless, the Widgery Report remained final.

In 1997 the Irish government concluded that, because of evidence produced by several new reports as well as other important material that had not been considered by the Widgery Report, it was time to look at the case again. This assessment was presented to the British government. On 29 January, 1998, British Prime Minister Tony Blair stated in the House of Commons: 'We believe that the weight of material now available is such that the events require re-examination. We believe that the only course that will lead to public confidence in the results of any further investigation is to set up a full-scale judicial inquiry into Bloody Sunday.' In the same year, a tribunal under the chairmanship of Lord Saville and assisted by three Commonwealth judges thus began fresh inquiries into the events of Bloody Sunday.

The findings of this tribunal, which is expected to deliver its report in 2004, will play an important role in the continuing peace process in Northern Ireland. Only when the truth about the events of Bloody Sunday has been established and openly acknowledged will both sides be able to lay this chapter of history to rest and look towards the future.

3 Where Was the Rule of Law? Dermot P.J. Walsh

Dermot Walsh is Professor of Law at University of Limerick. His 1997 report *The Bloody Sunday Tribunal of Inquiry* contributed to new evidence which led to a second official inquiry into the events of Bloody Sunday (cf. Info, p. 00). In the following excerpt from his more recent book *Bloody Sunday and the Rule of Law in Northern Ireland* (2000), Walsh describes the mood in Ireland and around the world immediately after Bloody Sunday.

Whatever the truth about these shootings there could be no doubting the profoundly serious and disturbing nature of their consequences. At one level there were the violent consequences. Rioting and shooting broke out in nationalist areas all over Northern Ireland as the nationalist community vented their anger at what they saw as mass murder inflicted on their community by the armed forces of the British crown. This violent reaction spilled over into the Republic of Ireland, where many street demonstrations resulted in attacks on British-owned commercial property and the burning of the British embassy in Dublin. Public protest marches and demonstrations were held in many cities around the world. Of greater long-term significance for the violence in Northern Ireland was the impact on IRA recruitment. Young men and women all over Ireland were queueing up to join the IRA in numbers that had not been witnessed before and have not been experienced since. Indeed Bloody Sunday might be cited, alongside internment and the H-Block hunger strikes, as one of the most influential events in provoking nationalist alienation from the state in Northern Ireland, and sustaining a long drawn-out and bloody war of insurrection which proved to be beyond the capacity of the state to quell.

> **'And the battle's just begun**
> **There's many lost, but tell me who has won**
> **The trench is dug within our hearts**
> **And mothers, children, brothers, sisters**
> **Torn apart**
> **Sunday, Bloody Sunday**
> **Sunday, Bloody Sunday'**
>
> ***– U2, 'Sunday Bloody Sunday'***

At a deeper level Bloody Sunday had implications for the very legitimacy of the state of Northern Ireland. [...] For many nationalists the events of Bloody Sunday sent out the stark message that the state would not even respect their right to life should they choose to engage in a show of public dissent against state policy. What they saw was the armed forces of the state engaging in mass killing and wounding in order to suppress a largely peaceful demonstration against the repressive policies of the state. In their eyes this was the ultimate proof of the illegitimacy of the state. Even in neutral circles the events of Bloody Sunday rocked public confidence in the rule of law and the integrity of government to the core. If there was any truth to the allegations being made about the actions of the army it was absolutely essential that they should be investigated quickly and in a manner which would persuade the sceptical that the inquiry was thorough, independent and impartial. If it discovered wrongdoing then it was equally essential that those responsible should be held accountable in an appropriate manner and the necessary remedial measures taken. Any failure to deliver on these requirements would simply compound the damage done to the rule of law and the integrity of the state in Northern Ireland. For nationalists it would be yet more confirmation, if more was needed, that the state was not capable of accommodating them

1. Walsh describes three consequences of the events of Bloody Sunday. Sum up each of these consequences in four or five words each and indicate whether they were of short-term or long-term significance.

2. According to the writer, what was 'absolutely essential' (ll. 56–57) after the events and why?

3. In your view, how subjective or objective is Walsh's perspective? Explain your answer using examples from the text.

4. It is the day after the events of Bloody Sunday and you have just heard the news. Write a letter to the editor of the *Belfast Telegraph* expressing your feelings about what has taken place and how you think it should be dealt with.

5. A second judicial inquiry into Bloody Sunday was set up in 1998 to learn the truth of what actually happened (cf. Info, p. 76). In groups, using the information in this book, the Internet and any other sources, research the differences in the way the Widgery and Saville Tribunals were/are conducted. Present your findings to the class.

7 *vent sth.:* show or express sth. (esp. an emotion) **26** *IRA* (abbr) = *Irish Republican Army:* militant organization of Irish nationalists founded with the aim of fighting for a united independent Ireland **28** *queue up* [kju:] (IrE, BE): wait in a line of people, cars, etc. in order to do or get sth. **31** *cite sth.* (fml): mention sth., refer to sth. **31–32** *internment:* imprisonment without trial (esp. during war or for political reasons) **32** *H-Block hunger strikes:* reference to the protest in 1981 by IRA prisoners who fought to keep their status as political prisoners; ten of them died after a long period of refusing to eat **34** *alienation* [ˌeɪliə'neɪʃn]: Entfremdung **36** *insurrection:* violent rebellion against a government **38** *to quell sth.:* stop sth. such as violent behaviour or protests **45** *dissent:* disapproval, opposition **48** *suppress sth.:* stop sth. from taking place, usu. by force, which is believed to threaten authority **52–54** *rock sth. to the core:* seriously damage sth. (esp. an attitude or a view towards sth.) **55** *allegation* (fml): Behauptung **59** *thorough* ['θʌrə ☆ 'θɜ:roʊ] (adj): done completely, with great attention to detail **60** *impartial:* neutral **65–66** *compound sth.:* make sth. bad become even worse **70** *accommodate sb.* (fml): accept sb.'s opinions and try to do what they want

4 8 a.m. News, Twelfth of July 1998 Paul Durcan

In the early-morning hours of Sunday, 12th July, 1998, three Catholic boys were killed when their family house was fire-bombed by a group of Protestant radicals. The murderous incident happened during the period of violence that usually accompanies the annual Orange Parades in the Northern Irish town of Portadown.

Protestant Orangemen are prevented from marching by a police barricade, 5 July, 1998.

i.m. Richard (10), Mark (9) and Jason (7) Quinn

'Adams Calls For Calm';
'Archbishop Cannot Find Words';
'Paisley Commiserates On Murdered Children'.

O God, why was I ever born?
Why cannot our Three Wise Musketeers
Instead of shooting the crap *en suite* –
Instead of locking themselves into
Their private lavatories,
Take tea together at Drumcree,
Hold hands, and
For the first time
In northwest European histor-ee
Move their bowels together?
Their gold-as-sunset bowels?
We poor Irish could do with a little
Excremental togetherness.

And God – what of Poor Old God?
Still young at heart, tramping the galaxies,
On the northwest seashore of northwest Europe
God picks up an orangey-greeny stone, peruses it,
Sobs to himself – *'Got Ireland here'* –
Spits on it, and over-arm
Bowls it into the bored-stiff ocean.
Ask my Granny – God weeps – *ask my Granny*

1. What is the meaning and significance of the quotes in ll. 2–4?
2. Explain what the speaker is saying in each stanza and summarize his overall message.
3. Analyse the language in the second and third stanzas (ll. 5–17, 18–25). How does it contribute to the tone of the poem?
4. Write an open letter to one of the three leaders – Adams, the Archbishop or Paisley – expressing your feelings on the incident and offering suggestions on how to solve the conflict. Alternatively, write a poem expressing your attitude toward the events in Portadown and/or the conflict in general.

Top to bottom: Gerry Adams, Archbishop Robin Eames and Reverend Ian Paisley. Above right: A firebombing by Protestants in Portadown, 11 July, 1990.

1 *i.m.* (abbr) = *in memory of* **2** *Adams = Gerry Adams* (born 1948): leader of Sinn Fein, the political party of the Irish Republican Army (IRA) **3** *Archbishop:* reference to Robin Eames (born 1937), Archbishop of the Church of Ireland **4** *Paisley = Reverend Ian Paisley* (born 1926): leader of the Ulster Union Democrats, a radical Protestant party **4** *commiserate on sth.:* show sb. sympathy when they are upset or disappointed about sth. **7** *shoot the crap* (infml): have an informal conversation **7** *en suite* (French): one after the other **9** *lavatory* (fml): toilet **10** *Drumcree:* area in Portadown, Northern Ireland, where violent clashes take place each year during the march of the Protestant Orangemen **14** *move your bowels* ['baʊəlz]: Stuhlgang haben **21** *peruse sth.* [pə'ruːz]: examine sth., esp. in a careful way **24** *bowl sth.:* throw sth. **24** *bored-stiff* (adj): completely bored **25** *Granny* (infml): grandmother

The Peace Process

The Irish Peace Process is the name given to the most recent attempts to achieve a political settlement to the civil conflict and political differences that divide the community in Northern Ireland. The Hume-Adams Initiative is seen by many as the beginning of this process. John Hume, Catholic leader of the Social Democratic and Labour Party (SDLP), and Gerry Adams, president of Sinn Féin (the political wing of the IRA) issued a statement in September 1993 which aimed at creating a peace process. Three months later, British Prime Minister John Major and Irish Taoiseach (Prime Minister) Albert Reynolds signed the Downing Street Declaration, which invited the IRA and loyalist paramilitary groups to join talks on the future of Northern Ireland in exchange for laying down their arms. Less than a year later, both the IRA and the combined loyalist groups announced a ceasefire. Following a long process of negotiation between the British and Irish governments and nearly all political parties, the historic Good Friday Agreement was signed on 10 April, 1998, and approved by the people of Northern Ireland and the Irish Republic in referendums on 22 May, 1998.

Top: David Trimble (left) and John Hume (right) celebrate the announcement of the Nobel Peace Prize. Bottom: Sinn Fein leader Gerry Adams announces the IRA's ceasefire.

The Agreement outlines new political structures in Northern Ireland, including a democratically elected Assembly that exercises executive and legislative authority, and re-defines relations between Northern Ireland and the Irish Republic, and between the Republic and the UK. Further, the Agreement includes sections on constitutional issues, human rights, decommissioning of arms, security, policing and prisoners.

The task of the Northern Ireland Assembly is to ensure that all sections of the community participate and work together in the running of the new political institutions and that all are equally protected. Assembly members are sworn to the principles of non-violence and democracy. The enormous political challenge of the Assembly is reflected in the fact that since 1998 it has been suspended several times in order to avoid a complete collapse. The main issues have been the decommissioning of arms, the establishment of an inclusive police force and an unwillingness to accept a power-sharing governing authority.

Despite initial optimism, the peace process remains incomplete and violence still continues. An unresolved issue is the Unionist Orange Order Parades in July and August, which celebrate the victory of (Protestant) William of Orange over (Catholic) James II in the 17th century. The Drumcree parade by the Portadown District Lodge of the Orange Order has been the main focal point of conflict (cf. this chapter, p. 80). On 15 August, 1998, dissident IRA extremists who were opposed to the peace process planted a car bomb in the city of Omagh which left 29 people dead and hundreds more seriously injured. It was the largest single loss of life in Northern Ireland since the troubles began. This incident and others might have ruined the peace process, but instead they have strengthened the resolve by the majority on both sides to seek a peaceful solution.

In December 1998, the SDLP leader John Hume and Ulster Unionist leader David Trimble were awarded the Nobel Peace Prize for their efforts to establish a lasting cooperation between the two opposing political parties.

5 NI Youth Welcome Peace

Mary Holland

The following is taken from an article which appeared in the *Irish Times* on 29th March, 2001.

A friend, who is a teacher in Derry, gave me a fascinating insight into the state of the Northern Ireland peace process. She was discussing options for third-level education with sixth-form pupils, with a view to filling out their applications to universities and other institutions.

One of the brightest students wanted to take a degree course in forensic science at a university in Britain, but with the firm intention of returning to Northern Ireland. My friend asked her what career opportunities would be open to her with such qualifications.

There was no hesitation in her reply. The girl plans to apply to join the new Northern Ireland Police Service with a view to working as a pathologist. She believes there will be great opportunities.

Nor was she alone in expressing this view. Another pupil, who plans to read law at university, also sees the new polic e service as a serious option for a fulfilling career.

A number of things about their discussion struck my friend. Both of these young women come from a strongly republican part of Derry. Yet there was no mention of the current political problems over the implementation of the Patten Report.

They were clearly confident the Northern Ireland Police Service will be in place by the time they are looking for jobs, and that it will be equally hospitable to nationalists and unionists. The fact they are both female and Catholic may give them a slight edge. [...]

For reasons I well understand, the press and the broadcasting media tend to concentrate on the crisis of the day or week, the continuing arguments over such issues as decommissioning and policing.

A visit to Derry last weekend has brought home once again the sea change that is under way.

It is difficult for people like myself, who lived close to the tragedy of 30 years of violence, to comprehend fully that there is a generation growing up who take the new order for granted. We should not relly be surprised. It is almost seven years since the first IRA ceasefire and the political landscape has been transformed.

The process hasn't been pain free. Those who have suffered in the conflict and still mourn loved ones lost in the violence cannot forget. Many others, and not only in the unionist community, find it difficult to accept how much things have changed.

But there is a deep desire to lay the past to rest. Its lessons must not be forgotten, but there has to be closure if people are to grasp the better future that is now on offer.

Sometimes, as with the sixth-form students described above, this process is almost unconscious.

1. Explain why the two students described in ll. 1–28 give the writer 'a fascinating insight into the state of the Northern Ireland peace process' (l. 1).

2. What are the two differing perspectives in Northern Ireland that Holland points out? How can each be explained?

3. Make a list of possible opportunities and challenges that you see for the future in Northern Ireland. Discuss your ideas with the class.

The Peace Statue
in Londonderry (Derry)

1 *Derry:* officially *Londonderry*, a town in Northern Ireland **4** *third-level education:* (in Ireland) university and college-level education **5** *sixth-form* (IrE, BE): Oberstufen- **9** *forensic science:* Gerichtsmedizin **15–16** *Northern Ireland Police Service:* police force formerly known as the Royal Ulster Constabulary (RUC), the name was changed and the organization restructured in November 2001 as a result of the Good Friday agreement (cf. *Info*, p. 82) and the Patten Report (cf. below, l. 28); the RUC was generally seen as a unionist force with few Catholic members (less than 10%) **20** *read sth.* (IrE, BE): study sth., esp. at university **22** *option* ['ɒpʃn ☆ 'ɑːp-]: possibility **28** *Patten Report:* official report published in September 1999 under the chairmanship of EU Commissioner Chris Patten which looks for ways to deal with conflicting issues and agendas between the nationalists and unionists **34** *slight edge:* small advantage **39** *decommissioning* (n): officially giving up the use of weapons; in Northern Ireland this is a particular issue with the Irish Republican Army (IRA), which has been slow in completely giving up its large arsenal **41** *sea change:* strong and noticeable change in a situation **46** *take sth. for granted:* etwas für selbstverständlich halten **58** *closure* ['kləʊʒə] (n): act of bringing sth. to an end or conclusion

6 Shades of Irishness Sammy Douglas

What it means to be 'Irish' is a particularly relevant question for the people of Northern Ireland. The following is taken from the book *Being Irish* (2000), a collection of personal reflections on Irish identity today. Sammy Douglas is a Belfast community development worker who is active in a wide range of voluntary work.

Sammy Douglas

I have fond memories of my late grandmother who grew up in the Grosvenor Road area of West Belfast. I remember her as a staunch Protestant and active unionist. Born in pre-partition Ireland, she was also proud of her Irish identity and she knew many Irish ballads off by heart.

When it came to my generation, I had absolutely no sense of Irishness. Growing up in the loyalist and unionist Sandy Row area of Belfast, everything around me affirmed a sense of being British. Red, white and blue painted kerbstones, royal photographs hung up on kitchen house walls and family links with the British forces going back decades, epitomised a proud British association and belonging. These 'traditions' helped to copper-fasten a passionate and emotional attachment to mainland Britain.

On the other hand, all things Irish were alien to me. I had learned from a very early age that their forces were always waiting along the border for an opportune time to take over Ulster and turn it into a Gaelic-speaking, priest-ridden, Roman Catholic republic. Irish 'neutrality' during the Second World War fuelled these anti-Irish attitudes and led to further alienation within the unionist community that I belonged to.

The negative feelings and hostility that I had harboured towards all things Irish were reinforced on my first day-trip across the border. As I arrived in the capital, tricolours, nuns and priests, huge chapels, an alien language and 'leprechaun pubs' confronted me. I felt like a stranger in a foreign country as I walked through the streets of 'dirty Dublin'. My sense of detachment from the Irish nation was compounded even more.

A traumatic experience a few years later was to challenge my long-held prejudices and enable me to examine an identity which had afforded me cultural and political security. In the 1970s, my sister was nearly killed after the IRA bombed the pub she was frequenting in Sandy Row. As I clawed through the demolished building looking for her, I was filled with raging anger and a sense of revenge. As an angry young man, I made a decision that had a major bearing on the direction of my life. I went to live in England.

When I arrived in Derby, East Midlands, any notion that I had of living in some sort of British Utopian state was soon dispelled. The people that I met didn't accept that I was from British Ulster. I was from Ireland and I was

'Paddy' to them. And I was no different from the 'Paddies' from the Falls Road, South Armagh, Dublin or Cork.

Like some of the ethnic minorities where I lived, I was racially abused at times. It was particularly bad after British soldiers were shot in Northern Ireland or when bombing atrocities were committed. It was hard to take and it began to shake my sense of identity to the core. It left me confused and bewildered.

As a result of these experiences, I made friends with Irish people from the Republic of Ireland. I came to realise that I had much in common with those, who, previously, I had perceived as foreigners. Although it was uncomfortable at first, I began to enjoy some aspects of Irish culture for the first time in my life. This included Irish literature, traditional music, dancing and songs. In cultural terms, this was a seismic shift for me. While I still considered myself an Ulsterman loyal to Britain, I gradually became more aware of my Irishness during my two-year stay.

Over the years I have retained the Irish angle to my identity, which I discovered during my time in England. The present peace process has created the conditions where unionists like myself can explore the Irish aspects of our identity in a relatively safe environment and in a way that does not threaten our Britishness. This is happening on a much wider scale than is generally recognised.

One only has to look at East Belfast where the 'writing is on the wall'. Murals such as St Patrick and Cuchullain are examples of an openness within our community to examine political 'hot potatoes'. And there are others. Irish and Ulster scots dancing survive alongside one another in some community centres while Irish jigs and songs are often played by loyalist flute bands.

But these changes are not just happening within the shadow of the giant cranes of Harland and Wolff shipyard. Through East Belfast Community Focus (funded by Co-operation Ireland), over 60 community organisations from East Belfast have travelled across the border to meet their counterparts. These exchange visits have taken place within this last year and have included organisations such as the British legion, Ulster Scots, loyalist prisoners' support groups and unionist politicians.

In conclusion, I am not trying to infer that many unionists have suddenly become Irish overnight or that there is a wee Irish person within us ready to jump out. Rather, there is a growing recognition within our community that an Ulsterman like myself, living in East Belfast, can be staunchly loyal and British but peculiarly Irish.

Above: Expressions of British loyalism in a Protestant neighbourhood in Belfast

3 staunch (adj): strong and loyal **4** pre-partition: before 1921, at which time Ireland was divided into Northern Ireland and the Irish Free State **9** Sandy Row [rəʊ ☆ roʊ]: Protestant neighbourhood in Belfast **10** affirm sth.: state or show that sth. is true **11** kerbstone: Bordsteinkante **14** epitomise sth. [ɪ'pɪtəmaɪz]: be a perfect example of sth. **16** copper-fasten sth. (IrE): strengthen, consolidate sth. **18** alien (adj) ['eɪliən]: fremd **20–21** priest-ridden (infml, derog): dominated by (Catholic) priests **26** tricolour: three-coloured flag, (here) the Irish flag **26–27** leprechaun ['leprəkɔːn]: (in Irish stories) creature like a little man with magic powers (cf. illustration, p. 17) **28** detachment: state of not being involved in sth. in an emotional or a personal way **33–34** claw through sth.: move through sth. (here, the ruins of a building) with great effort and difficulty **36** have a bearing on sth.: have important consequences for sth. **38** dispel sth. (fml): make sth., esp. a feeling or belief, go away or disappear **40** Paddy (infml., derog): person from Ireland **41** Falls Road: Catholic neighbourhood in Belfast **41** Armagh [ˌɑː'mɑː]: town in Northern Ireland (cf. the map, inside cover) **42** Cork: town in the Irish Republic (cf. the map, inside cover) **44** abuse sb. [ə'bjuːz]: say rude or offensive things to or about sb. **46** atrocity [ə'trɒsəti ☆ ə'trɑː-]: terrible, cruel and violent act, esp. in a war **49** bewildered [bɪ'wɪldəd] (adj): verwirrt **59** seismic shift: movement of the earth caused by an earthquake; (here) enormous, sudden change
73 mural ['mjuːrəl]: large painting on a wall
73 St Patrick (?385–461): national saint of Ireland
74 Cuchullain [kuː'kʌlɪn]: in Celtic mythology a legendary hero of Ulster **76–77** Ulster scots: of the protestant Ulster community whose ancestors came from Scotland **81–82** Harland and Wolff: large shipbuilding company in Belfast; its two giant cranes are a city landmark, often referred to as 'David and Goliath' **91** infer (v): conclude, imply **98** peculiar [pɪ'kjuːliə] (adj): strange, odd

1. Sammy Douglas mentions the 'Red, white and blue painted kerbstones' (l. 11) of the strongly loyalist neighbourhood he grew up in. Imagine the neighbourhoods of your hometown were divided in a similar way between different groups. Why might people do this and what might be its effect?
2. Describe the experience which led Sammy Douglas to open himself up to Irish culture and heritage.
3. According to Douglas, what particular effect has the peace process had on members of both communities?
4. The text points to another kind of 'being Irish' that is quite different from the common image we have of Irish people and culture. Explain this experience in general in your own words.
5. Douglas writes about the cross-cultural experience that he and other Irish have had within Ireland. To what extent do you think the cultural encounter between Germans since the fall of the Berlin Wall has been similar?
6. Imagine you are Sammy Douglas living in England as a young man. Write a letter home to your sister in Belfast describing your experiences and feelings and the changes you are going through.

Acknowledgements

Texts **I/1** By Gisela Holfter. Reprinted by permission. **I/2** From the website of the German Federal Foreign Office **I/3** From 'Brussels Seen as Farmers' Golden Calf', *The Irish Times*, September 30, 1998. 'How the Germans Found Their Lebensraum into the West', by Anne Lucey, *The Cork Examiner*, October 3, 1998.

II/1 'Celtic Tiger' by Jane Black, *ZDNet*, November 27, 2000. **II/2** From *Ireland and the Irish – Portait of a Changing Society*, by John Ardagh (Penguin, Harmondsworth, 1994). **II/3** 'The Tiger' by Vincent Byrne, from *Electric Acorn Nr. 9* (Dublin Writers' Workshop, Dublin, 2000).

III/2 From *Angela's Ashes* by Frank McCourt (HarperCollins, London, 1996). **III/3** 'The Sirens Voice' by Chisty Moore from *Traveller* (Columbia/Sony, 1999). **III/4** From *A Part of Ireland Now* by Andy Pollock and Derek Speirs (Refugee Agency, Department of Foreign Affairs, Ireland, 1997). **III/5** From *The Irish Times*, May 9, 2000. **III/6** From 'Accusations about Stealing Their Jobs', *The Irish Times on the Web*, June 17, 2000.

IV/2 From *Goodbye to Catholic Ireland* by Mary Kenny (New Island, Dublin, 2000). **IV/3** From *The Heather Blazing* by Colm Toíbín (Bloomsbury Classics, London, 1995). **IV/4** From *The Snapper* by Roddy Doyle (Vintage, London, 1991).

V/2 From *Eureka Street* by Robert McLiam Wilson (Vintage, London, 1996). **V/3** From *Bloody Sunday and the Rule of Law in Northern Ireland* by Dermot P. J. Walsh (Macmillan, London, 2000). **V/4** From *Greetings to Our Friends in Brazil* (Harvill Press, London, 1999). **V/5** From 'NI Young Welcome Dividends of Peace', *The Irish Times on the Web*, March 29, 2001. **V/6** From *Being Irish* by Paddy Logue (Oak Tree Press, 2001).

Illustrations Action Press, Hamburg: p. 50 (top left, © Rex Features); Agentur Focus, Hamburg: cover (city, © Gideon Mendel/Network), pp. 6 (Dell Computer factory, © Gideon Mendel/Network), 20 (© G. Hänel & U. Thomas), 21 (city and business people/pub, © Gideon Mendel/Network), 22 (top left, © Gideon Mendel/Network); American Forces Information Centre: p. 17; AP Photo: pp. 25 (backdrop, © Andreas Pechar), 27 (© Remy de la Mauvinière), 73 (bottom, © Peter Morrison), 74 (© Max Nash), 79 (© Peter Morrison), 80 (© Peter Morrison); The Art Archive, London: p. 36 (top); Belfast Visitor & Convention Bureau: p. 6 (Royal Avenue); © Volkhard Binder, Berlin: cover inside, map; © Buena Vista Home Entertainment, Inc.: pp. 64-65 (all); © Cyril Byrne Photo: p. 46; Cinetext: p. 54 (top); Corbis: pp. 6 (statue near abbey, © Tim Thompson, barricade, © Alain Le Garsmeur), 21 (shopping center, © Richard Cummins), 32-33 (row of cottages, © E.O. Hoppé), 50-51 (© Tim Thompson), 52 (top, © Sygma/Sophie Bassouls); Corel-Library: pp. 38-39, 52-53, 54 (bottom), 55; defd-pwe Verlag GmbH/Kinoarchiv: p. 32 (bottom); Dpa-Bildarchiv: pp. 25 (bottom left), 77 (all, © UPI), 81 (bottom left, © Paul Faith), 82 (bottom, © Penny); Dpa-Fotoreport: pp. 11 (top right, © Tim Brakemeier, bottom left, © Bernd Settnik), 12-13 (bottom, © Peter Förster), 13 (right, © Tom Mallsa), 73 (top right, © PA Faith), 81 (top left, © Paul Faith); © Sammy Douglas, Belfast: p. 85; 'Mother Ireland' and 'Mother Ulster' by Rita Duffy, pp. 70-71 (© Rita Duffy, Belfast); © Emmwood (= John Musgrave-Wood): p. 16; 'Madonna Irlanda' by Michael Farrel, 1977, p. 49 (© Dublin City Gallery, The Hugh Lane/Meg Early-O'Farrel); Das Fotoarchiv, Essen: pp. 86-87 (photo and backdrop, © Sebastian Bolesch); gettyimages/Stone: p. 6 (sheep farmer, © Mark Joseph); © Harper Collins Publishers: p. 32 (top left); 'Exiles' by Patrick Hennessy, 1943, p. 30 (© Dublin City Gallery, The Hugh Lane); Christopher Hill Photographic, Belfast: pp. 6-7, 18, 56; Gisela Holfter, Limerick: pp. 8-10 (all); Image Bank, Berlin: p. 62; The Irish Image Collection: cover (landscape with church, © Liam Blake), pp. 6 (main street Avoca, Ballykissangel), 12 (top left, © Tim Hannen), 14-15, 15 (right), 57 (top right), 58-59 (photo and backdrop, © Richard Cummins), 72 (© Chris Hill), 83 (top, © Chris Hill), 84; Mauritius: pp. 47 (© age), 53 (top, © Nonstock); Pacemaker Press International Ltd., Belfast: p. 76; PA Photos, London: pp. 57 (all except top right), 83 (bottom); photo oikoumene, Geneva: cover ('Hands across a divided Derry' monument, © Peter Williams/WCC); Rita Preuß, Berlin: p. 21 (street in Dublin); REUTERS/E-LANCE MEDIA: pp. 75 (© Paul McErlane), 81 (top, middle left, © Kieran Doherty), 82 (top); © David Rooney: pp. 18-19; © Derek Speirs, Dublin: pp. 22 (bottom left), 36 (bottom), 40-41 (all), 44-45; © Martyn Turner: pp. 23, 26, 28-29, 43.